Virginia Woolf
Interviews and Recollections

VIRGINIA WOOLF

Interviews and Recollections

Edited by

J. H. STAPE

University of Iowa Press, Iowa City

Contents

Part VII   Woolf Remembered   **169**

Preface

'Invitations to write something keep coming in, but I am refusing – I don't want to write without being funny, and I don't feel funny', wrote E. M. Forster to Clive Bell shortly after Virginia Woolf's death. Whatever their feelings, others accepted such invitations, and as early as May 1941, Cyril Connolly's *Horizon* published a cluster of reminiscences and obituary tributes by distinguished writers and friends of Woolf. Over the next few decades others recalled their association with her, and in 1972, drawing on these as well as on the memorial issue of *Horizon*, Joan Russell Noble edited a highly informative collection entitled *Recollections of Virginia Woolf.*

With two exceptions, the present volume has avoided reprinting reminiscences that Noble printed. Its emphasis falls mainly on the immediate impressions of Virginia Woolf's contemporaries although it also includes a few full dress portraits. It also aims to offer new material and to supplement the large body of already available writing about Woolf's life both by herself and others. Thus the present collection offers perspectives on a variety of Woolf's activities – her famous and influential lectures at Cambridge, her role in the Hogarth Press and her presence in the social and literary world of her day. Also represented is the private Virginia Woolf – the sister, wife and intimate friend – a figure that the publication of her diary and letters has made better known to present-day readers than to many of her contemporaries.

There has been no lack of material to draw upon, and it is hoped that this collection will engender new insights as well as confirm or alter received ideas about Woolf's character and personality. Certainly, the view of her, fostered in some quarters during her lifetime, as a neurotically withdrawn and overly delicate individual has by now been long revised. On the other hand, her own and her circle's fascination with 'lives' and biography and her circumspect attitude towards any final vision of 'a life' ought caution against any single appropriation of hers.

A coherent view of so extraordinarily chameleon a temperament and talent is, of course, impossible. If Lily Briscoe in *To the Lighthouse* needs 'fifty pairs of eyes' to take in a woman as simple as Mrs Ramsay, even more pairs are desirable for focusing on a Virginia Woolf. The difficulty of a balanced viewpoint for some of her memoirists, a demanding enough task at the best of times, was compounded by the enthusiasm with which she sometimes donned a mask and by conversation whose notorious brilliance veered at moments towards the flamboyant, the wildly inaccurate or the cruel as her mood shifted or as madness, however distantly, threatened.

As with any collection of this kind there are necessarily disappointments and lacunae. Woolf herself gave no interviews although her multi-volume diary amply offers her changing thoughts about the shape and direction of her art and life. The nature and extent of recollections of her are, as might be expected, of varying authority and quality, and those written some time after her death share problems common to the remembering imagination – inexactitude, exaggeration and invention. While these at least might be discreetly addressed by annotation, there is the disappointment of permission fees being beyond budget in a few instances.

The organisation of the recollections gathered together here attempts thematic coherence within a roughly chronological framework. The opening sections concentrate on Virginia Woolf as individual and as writer and include extracts from the diaries of contemporaries. The volume's middle section centres on facets of Woolf's involvements with friends and other writers, especially with the Bloomsbury Group, and focuses on her connections with the Hogarth Press, which she and her husband Leonard Woolf established. The closing sections group together pen portraits and obituary appreciations, presenting Virginia Woolf from the vantage point of retrospect and evaluation.

Acknowledgements

The editor and publishers would like to thank the following for their kind permission to use copyright material:

Professor Joanne Trautmann Banks and Mr Nigel Nicolson, for 'A Talk with Nigel Nicolson'.

Professor Quentin Bell, for permission to quote letters in the Charleston Papers.

The Berg Collection, New York Public Library, Astor, Lenox and Tilden Foundations, for the extracts from the diaries of the late Sydney Waterlow and for the travel diary of the late Vita Sackville-West.

Curtis Brown & John Farquharson Ltd, for the contribution by the late Elizabeth Bowen to 'The Death of Virginia Woolf'.

Cambridge University Press, for the extracts from *A Newnham Anthology*.

Dr H. P. Cecil, for 'A Note on Virginia Woolf' by the late David Cecil.

The Charleston Trust, for 'Memories of the Hogarth Press' by Elizabeth Hepworth.

Chatto & Windus Ltd, for 'Virginia Woolf' by the late Clive Bell and for the extract from *Unfinished Business: A Memoir* by the late John Houseman.

Constable Publishers Ltd, for the extract from *Middle Age, 1885–1932* by the late G. E. Easdale.

Mrs Angelica Garnett, for 'Notes on Virginia's Childhood' by the late Vanessa Bell and for her contribution to 'The Death of Virginia Woolf'.

HarperCollins Publishers Ltd, for the extracts from *Diaries and Letters 1930–1939* and *Diaries and Letters 1939–1945* by the late Harold Nicolson.

Sir Rupert Hart-Davis, for the extract from *Autobiography* by the late William Plomer.

David Higham Associates Ltd, for 'Working with Virginia Woolf' by the late John Lehmann, for the extract from *Taken Care Of: An Autobiography* by the late Edith Sitwell, and for the extract from *Laughter in the Next Room* by the late Osbert Sitwell and for his letter to Vanessa Bell.

Mrs Olive M. Kennedy, for the extracts from *A Boy at the Hogarth Press* by the late Richard Kennedy.

Listener Publications Ltd, for 'The Death of Virginia Woolf', 'Working with Virginia Woolf' by the late John Lehmann, 'Virginia Woolf: A Tribute' by Stephen Spender, and 'Virginia Woolf: Writer and Personality' by the late Leonard Woolf.

Longman Group UK Ltd, for the extract from *Ethel Smyth: A Biography* by Christopher St John.

Mr Nigel Nicolson, for the travel diary of the late Vita Sackville-West.

Mrs Trekkie Parsons, for 'Virginia Woolf: Writer and Personality' by the late Leonard Woolf.

Murray Pollinger, literary agent, for the extract from *Ottoline at Garsington: Memoirs of Lady Ottoline Morrell*.

Reed Books Services, for 'Virginia' by the late Enid Bagnold.

Mr George Sassoon, for the extract from *Siegfried Sassoon Diaries 1923–1925*.

The Spectator, for 'Virginia Woolf' by the late Rose Macaulay.

Sir Stephen Spender, for his 'Virginia Woolf: A Tribute'.

Abner Stein Ltd, for the extract from *Unfinished Business: A Memoir* by the late John Houseman.

The late Janet Vaughan, for her 'Some Bloomsbury Memories'.

A. P. Watt Ltd, on behalf of the executors of the estate of David Garnett, for 'Virginia Woolf' by the late David Garnett.

The following copyright credits are also made:

The extracts from Gerald Brenan's *Personal Record: 1920–1972* and *South from Granada*; © Gerald Brenan 1974 and 1957; reprinted by permission of Margaret Hanbury, literary agent, on behalf of the estate of Gerald Brenan, 27 Walcot Square, London SE11 4UB.

The extract from a letter of E. M. Forster to Clive Bell [April 1941]; © the Provost and Scholars of King's College, Cambridge, 1994.

'Virginia Woolf' from *Great Friends: Portraits of Seventeen Writers* by David Garnett; © David Garnett 1979; reprinted by permission of Atheneum Publishers (US rights), an imprint of Macmillan Publishing Company.

'Virginia Stephen' by Duncan Grant; © Duncan Grant estate 1978; reprinted by permission of Henrietta Garnett.

The extract from *Memories* by Frances Partridge; © Frances Partridge 1981; first published by Victor Gollancz 1981; reprinted by permission of Rogers, Coleridge & White, Ltd.

The extract from *The Land Unknown* by Kathleen Raine; © Kathleen Raine 1975; reprinted by permission of Hamish Hamilton, Ltd.

The extracts from *The Diary of Beatrice Webb*, vol. IV; reprinted by permission of Virago Press and Harvard University Press, Cambridge, Mass.; editorial matter and arrangement © 1983, 1984 Norman and Jeanne Mackenzie; the Diary of Beatrice Webb, the Passfield Papers © 1983, 1984 the London School of Economics and Political Science.

'Une femme étincelante et timide' by the late Marguerite Yourcenar; © Editions Gallimard Bibliothèque de la Pléiade 1982.

Whilst every effort has been made to locate owners of copyright, in a few cases this has been unsuccessful. The editor and publishers apologise for any infringement of copyright and shall be glad to include any necessary corrections in subsequent printings.

Thanks for answering enquiries and for providing information and advice are due to Professor Quentin Bell, Dr Laurence Davies, Mr Raymond Gauthier, Professor James M. Haule, Mrs Atsuko Hayakawa, Ms Kate Perry (Archivist, Girton College, Cambridge), Professor S. P. Rosenbaum and the Society of Authors. I am grateful to Ms Izumi Iwasaki, Ms Masumi Saito, Professor Syun Tutiya and, especially, Mr Seiichiro Kanamoto for technical assistance.

A Note on the Text

In the selections, spelling errors in the original have been silently corrected. A writer's spellings and usages have been retained except for the omission of the terminal point in abbreviations such as Dr and Mr.

In the case of material published here for the first time, paragraphing and punctuation have been styled to conform to standard practice. While their integrity has been respected, such pieces have, where necessary, been subject to minor editorial alteration to facilitate reading.

Titles of books, plays, ships, operas and pictures are printed in italics, those of short stories in quotation marks. Unspaced points (...) indicate ellipses in the original while spaced points (. . .) indicate an editorial omission within a selection.

In cases where titles have been supplied or altered the original title appears in full in the publication information.

Quotations from Woolf's works have been altered to conform to a published text, and for ease of reference Penguin's 'Twentieth-Century Classics' editions have usually been cited. Quotations from Woolf's letters have been altered to conform to the Hogarth Press's edition (see below). Misquotations from material other than Woolf's works have been silently corrected.

The notes normally identify individuals on first mention except where the person is an author of a memoir printed herein. Dates for events in Woolf's life and the publication dates of her writings are found in the Chronology.

The abbreviation *Diary* refers to *The Diary of Virginia Woolf*, edited by Anne Olivier Bell with the assistance of Andrew McNeillie (5 vols, Hogarth Press, 1977–84), and *Letters* to *The Letters of Virginia Woolf*, edited by Nigel Nicolson and Joanne Trautmann (6 vols, Hogarth Press, 1975–80).

A Virginia Woolf Chronology

1882   (*25 Jan.*) Adeline Virginia Stephen, third child of Leslie Stephen and Julia Duckworth, born at 22 Hyde Park Gate, London.

— 1895   Woolf's mother dies. First mental breakdown.

1896   Travels in France with her sister Vanessa.

1904   Woolf's father dies. First published essay and review.

1905   Begins teaching evening courses at Morley College (until 1907). Starts to review regularly in the *Guardian* and *Times Literary Supplement*. Travels in Spain and Portugal.

1906   Visits Greece. Woolf's brother Thoby dies from typhoid contracted during the sojourn.

1907   Begins first version ('Melymbrosia' version) of *The Voyage Out*.

1908   Travels in Italy with Vanessa and Clive Bell.

1909   Visits Florence. Attends the Bayreuth Festival.

1910   Participates in the '*Dreadnought* Hoax'.

1911   Travels to Turkey.

1912   Marries Leonard Woolf. Travels in France, Spain and Italy.

1913   Attempts suicide after a summer of ill-health.

— 1915   *The Voyage Out* published. Struggles with madness.

1917   Founds the Hogarth Press with Leonard Woolf. *The Mark on the Wall* published.

1919   *Kew Gardens* and *Night and Day* published. Establishes country home, Monk's House, at Rodmell, Sussex.

1921   *Monday or Tuesday* published. Meets Vita Sackville-West.

1922   *Jacob's Room* published.

1923   Visits Gerald Brenan in Spain.

1925   *The Common Reader* (1st series) and *Mrs Dalloway* published.

1927   *To the Lighthouse* published. Travels in Italy.

1928   *To the Lighthouse* awarded the Femina-Vie Heureuse Prize. *Orlando: A Biography* published. Lectures on 'Women & Fiction' at Cambridge.

1929   *A Room of One's Own* published. Travels in Germany.

1930   The Hogarth Press issues the Uniform Edition of Woolf's novels.

1931 *The Waves* published. Travels in France.
1932 *The Common Reader* (2nd series) published.
1933 *Flush: A Biography* published.
1937 *The Years* published.
1938 *Three Guineas* published.
1940 *Roger Fry: A Biography* published.
1941 Drowns herself in the River Ouse, Sussex (*28 Mar.*). *Between the Acts*, begun in 1939, posthumously published.
1942 *The Death of the Moth and Other Essays* published.
1944 *A Haunted House and Other Short Stories* published.
1947 *The Moment and Other Essays* published.
1950 *The Captain's Death Bed and Other Essays* published.
1953 *A Writer's Diary* published.
1958 *Granite and Rainbow* published.
1965 *Contemporary Writers* published.
1976 *Moments of Being* and *Freshwater* published.
1977 *Books and Portraits* published.

Part I
Woolf Observed

Notes on Virginia's Childhood*

VANESSA BELL

The more I see of children – and I am thankful to say I do manage to see more of them now – the more I realise that their world is quite unlike ours. It is so different from ours that, it seems to me, to describe it needs a peculiar kind of imagination and understanding. And I think any real account of childhood would necessarily be long, for how much happens in an hour or a day of a child's life, and what changes come in a year!

We were all so near in age that I cannot be very sure that many of my memories have any sort of truth. Why do I see her so clearly, a very rosy chubby baby, with bright green eyes, sitting in a high chair at the nursery table, drumming impatiently for her breakfast? She cannot have been more than two, and I therefore only about four and a half. But it is a vivid memory to me. How worried I was too, not much later, because she couldn't speak clearly; I feared she would never do so, which would certainly have been a misfortune. That cannot have lasted long, for we were not very old when speech became the deadliest weapon as used by her. When Thoby[1] and I were angry with each other or with her, we used good straightforward abuse, or perhaps told tales if we felt particularly vindictive. How did she know that to label me 'The Saint' was far more effective, quickly reducing me to the misery of sarcasm from the grown-ups as well as the nursery world? One was vaguely aware that it was no good trying to retort in kind. No, our only revenge for such injuries, Thoby's and mine, was to make her, as we said, 'purple with rage'. I don't remember how we did this, I only remember watching her colour mount till it was the most lively flaming red – and then I suppose nurses interfered. Was it altogether painful to her? I am not sure.

---

* *Notes on Virginia's Childhood: A Memoir*, ed. Richard J. Schaubeck, Jr (New York: Frank Hallman, 1974).

I see us as children nearly always in the two nurseries almost at the top of the tall house in Hyde Park Gate. There we spent about ten months of the year, and in spite of the delights of our Cornish Home[2] I used sometimes to feel it almost unbearable so seldom to be in a wood in the spring – in the early summer, never. (Brighton was the nearest we usually got to such joys, and I have hated it ever since in consequence.) Not that we were often bored even in London; Kensington Gardens was comparatively wild in those days, and in the long grass between the Flower Walk and the Round Pond we had once had the thrill of finding the deserted corpse of a dog – a little black dog. Then four children can make a good deal of amusement and trouble for each other. Perhaps I should say three, for Adrian[3] was still a baby or a delicate little boy, and Thoby the brother both Virginia and I adored. She has described him so fully that I need say nothing.[4] But he and I had had an intimate friendship before she came on the scene, doing everything together, and later, though life was more interesting and exciting, it was also less easy. Even then she had the faculty of suddenly being able to create an atmosphere of tense thundery gloom. I think she always had this – perhaps it's a Stephen characteristic – but I had not been aware of it before she produced it. Suddenly the sky was overcast, and I in the gloom. It would last for endless ages – so it seemed to a child – and then go. But it was I who had been in the gloom – not the other two – and I suppose, though I cannot remember ever feeling it at the time, that it was simply the result of two little females and a male. Or was it something different and part of her temperament?

Children are jealous little creatures, and brothers and sisters in a large family have one great disadvantage over only children. No one ever says how nice Mary is or how lovely Jane, but always Mary is nicer than Jane and Jane prettier than Mary. It's inevitable, and comparisons are the easiest form of criticism, no doubt, but it may lead to trouble. I don't remember being jealous of the fact that her appearance and her talk had obviously the greatest success with the grown-ups. They laughed at her jokes but so did we all, and probably I was as much aware as anyone of her brilliance and loveliness to look at. She reminded me always of a sweet pea of a special flame colour. But then there was the unfortunate question of our godparents. We hadn't been baptised, but all the same we had godparents of a kind. Mine were very dull, a decrepit old cousin in Ceylon and Lady Vaughan Williams, the judge's wife, whom I couldn't bear. But Virginia had the American ambassador, James Russell Lowell,[5] a great friend of our parents who was quite an important figure to us. He used to produce his chain purse and pull out of it 3d bits for each of us except Virginia, who got 6d. That wasn't very important though rather marked, but what really roused our jealousies was his giving her a bird, a real live bird in a cage. I suppose the poor man would have been much surprised had he known what evil passions he had caused.

One of the two nurseries in which we lived was the day, the other the night nursery, and in this we four children and a nurse slept and had our baths and did all else in what I think must by modern standards have been a very unhealthy atmosphere. Was the window ever open at night? I doubt it. There was a lovely bright fire to go to bed by, coal, food, hot water and babies being carried up many times a day. We were very snug, if stuffy, and of course told stories in bed. The only one I remember was a serial which went on night after night. The characters were real ones, those of our next door neighbours, the Dilke family, who we mocked for not being able to pronounce the letter R. The story always began by saying in an affected drawl, 'Clemente, dear child'. Virginia then took the part of Clemente and the séance would begin. The plot consisted in the discovery under their nursery floor of immense stores of gold. It then went on to describe the wonderful things they could buy in consequence, especially the food, which was unlimited, though mostly consisting of not then very ruinous eggs and bacon – our favourite dish. But as we got sleepier our ideas got vaguer, and vast oceans of wealth and sleep seemed to overwhelm one. The fire flickered, one by one we dropped off to sleep, and presently 'Clemente dear child' gave no answer. The story had to wait till next night. It was in these two nurseries that we all had whooping cough, for of course there was no question of one alone getting any infectious disease. I believe children on the whole love being ill, but that particular disease did seem to last a very long time. Probably the treatment was completely wrong; anyhow I think we stayed indoors most of the time and had special foods and lots of medicines and in the end emerged four little skeletons and were sent to Bath for a change. The rest of us quickly recovered, but it seemed to me that Virginia was different. She was never again a plump and rosy child and, I believe, had actually entered into some new layer of consciousness rather abruptly, and was suddenly aware of all sorts of questions and possibilities hitherto closed to her. I remember one evening as we were jumping about naked, she and I, in the bathroom, she suddenly asked me which I liked best, my father or mother. Such a question seemed to me rather terrible; surely one ought not to ask it. I felt certain Thoby would have snubbed the questioner. However, being asked, one had to reply, and I found I had little doubt as to my answer. 'Mother', I said, and she went on to explain why she, on the whole, preferred my father. I don't think, however, her preference was quite as sure and simple as mine. She had considered both critically and had more or less analysed her feelings for them which I, at any rate consciously, had never attempted. This seemed to begin an age of much freer speech between us. If one could criticise one's parents, what or whom could one not criticise? Dimly some freedom of thought and speech seemed born, created by her question.

Before Thoby went to school at the age of ten, he and I had done all our lessons together, but after that it was Virginia and I who shared ours. My mother taught us Latin, French and history – not very well, I think, and I am sure most mistakenly, both on her own account and on ours. What a relief it was when for a short time she went abroad with my father and we had a harmless, ordinary little governess. It is much too nerve-wracking to be taught by one's parents. But my father's lessons in arithmetic were the worse of the two, and how the poor man endured them I cannot think. Thoby was the only one of his children whom it can have been a pleasure to teach. Virginia all her life added up on her fingers and I am very little better. She always said that she had had no education, and I am inclined to agree with her, if by education is meant learning things out of books. If she had none, however, I had less, for she did at least teach herself or get herself taught Greek, and was given books to read by my father which may, for all I know, have had educational value.

However there were also classes. Music naturally, since we were girls, had to be drummed into us, and the piano mistress succeeded in reducing us to complete boredom. The singing class, on the other hand, had its amusing side in the shape of other children. Miss Mills, a well-known teacher of the tonic sol-fa system in those days, was discovered by us to be intensely religious. So when one day she asked very seriously if any of us knew the meaning of Good Friday, Virginia began to giggle. Of course we hadn't the slightest idea, being little heathens. But when the prize girl of the class, a serious creature with a hooked nose and a fringe and the astonishing name of Pensa Filly, stepped forward and said something (I suppose accurately) about our Lord being crucified on that day, it was too much and Virginia had to be hurriedly banished, shrieking with laughter. It amused her very much too when Connor O'Brien, a fiery little Irish boy, burst into floods of tears because he wasn't top of the class; but when that happened it was he, kicking and screaming, who had to be removed by his shamefaced mother.

Then there was the dancing class with the celebrated Mrs Wordsworth in black satin. She had a stick and a glass eye at which she dabbed perpetually with a lace pocket handkerchief, and she croaked like a raven and made all the little girls jump up and down in a frenzy. But we were bored and sometimes retired to the W.C. and spent as long as we dared there. I don't know what the sixty or seventy other girls did meanwhile.

I cannot remember a time when Virginia did not mean to be a writer and I a painter. It was a lucky arrangement, for it meant that we went our own ways and one source of jealousy at any rate was absent.

Our happiest afternoons were spent in a small room handed over to us, opening from the large double drawing room. It was a cheerful little room, almost entirely made of glass, with a skylight, windows all along one side looking on to the back garden, a window cut in the wall between it and the drawing room, and a door (also half window) opening into the drawing room. Also another door by which one could retreat to the rest of the house. In this room we used to sit, I painting and she reading aloud. We read most of the Victorian novelists in this way, and I can still hear much of George Eliot and Thackeray in her voice. From this room too we could spy on the grown-ups. Naturally we produced a family newspaper, *The Hyde Park Gate News*. Virginia wrote most of it, and it lasted four or five years, I believe – I have copies of it from the years 1891 and 1895. She was very sensitive to criticism and the good opinion of the grown-ups. I remember putting the paper on the table by my mother's sofa while they were at dinner, and then creeping quietly into the little room to look through the window and hear the criticism. As we looked, she trembling with excitement, we could see my mother's lamplit

figure quietly sitting near the fire, my father on the other side
with his lamp, both reading. Then she noticed the paper, picked
it up, began to read. We looked and listened hard for some comment. 'Rather clever, I think', said my mother, putting the paper
down without apparent excitement. But it was enough to thrill
her daughter; she had had approval and been called clever, and
our eavesdropping was rewarded. I think it must have been a
good deal later that she sent a short story to *Tit Bits*, keeping it a
deadly secret from all but me. *Tit Bits* was our favourite weekly,
which we used to buy together with 3d worth of Fry's Chocolate, taking both to Kensington Gardens to read and eat together,
lying in the grass under the trees on summer afternoons. The
story was refused – as far as I remember, it was a wildly romantic account of a young woman on a ship – and the secret kept till
this day.[6]

NOTES

Vanessa Bell, née Stephen (1879–1961), painter, Virginia Woolf's sister.
This paper was delivered to the Memoir Club after Woolf's death.

1. Thoby Stephen (1880–1906).
2. Talland House, St Ives, Cornwall, where the Stephens summered
from 1882 to 1894. The house is recollected in *To the Lighthouse*.
3. Adrian Stephen (1883–1948).
4. Woolf drew on him for Jacob Flanders of *Jacob's Room* and for
Percival in *The Waves*. See also 'A Sketch of the Past', *Moments of Being:
Unpublished Autobiographical Writings of Virginia Woolf*, ed. Jeanne
Schulkind (Brighton: Sussex University Press, 1976).
5. James Russell Lowell (1819–91), essayist, poet and editor, also a
professor at Harvard and statesman.
6. Apparently an embryonic version of *The Voyage Out*.

Cousin Virginia*

DAME JANET VAUGHAN

When I was asked about my memories of Bloomsbury, I got out my mother's tattered old scrapbook. I found faded photographs of Leslie Stephen and Julia standing out in the snow at Davos, where they were staying with my grandfather John Addington Symonds,[1] enjoying the early days of 'winter sports'. There were photographs also of Leslie Stephen seated in his arm chair in the Hyde Park study and a very lovely one of Julia looking out of the same window as she pulled aside the curtain to let the light fall full on her face. Julia was my father's aunt and Leslie Stephen a long-standing friend of John Addington Symonds. My mother, Madge Symonds, his daughter, first met my father, William Vaughan, in the gloomy house in Hyde Park Gate and also at St Ives.[2] Madge was the early great love of Virginia, who described her as Sally Beaton in *Mrs Dalloway*. So I grew up with a background of a pre-Bloomsbury world. As a child, I can remember the excitement of the arrival of Virginia and Cordelia[3] in a painted horse-drawn caravan to stay with us in the West Riding of Yorkshire. Why a caravan and where they were going remains obscure.

My father, now a public school headmaster, disapproved of the way the Stephen girls conducted their lives after they moved from Hyde Park Gate. This disapproval was confirmed at the time of the Great Hoax, February 1910, when '5 men and a young woman who, with the aid of elaborate make-ups passed themselves off as Abyssinian princes, an interpreter and a representative of the Foreign Office, were accorded royal honours and shown all over the mighty battleship by Admiral Sir William May and the *Dreadnought* officers'.[4] My mother Madge Vaughan cut the picture out of *The Times* on 16th February and stuck it in the family scrapbook, marking Virginia and Adrian by an X and their

---

* 'Some Bloomsbury Memories', *Charleston Newsletter*, no. 12 (September 1985) pp. 20–2.

names. I have it still. Perhaps it should come back to Monk's House or Charleston?[5]

Later there was further cause for his disapproval, an occasion which I well remember, when my mother went to stay at Charleston just after Angelica[6] was born and came back devoted as ever to Vanessa and Virginia, but bewildered by the domestic chaos she found; beds never made up, meals never on time. However, the links with the Stephens were maintained, and when I went to London as a medical student Virginia was welcoming. I lived in 19 Taviton Street where Francis Birrell, my husband's great friend, had his bookshop with David Garnett, and I kept my bicycle in the passage of the Hogarth Press house in Tavistock Square.[7]

At the time of the General Strike,[8] Hilda Matheson, as secretary to Lady Astor, was organising concerts for the strikers and the unemployed in empty churches and other halls. Why this was done I don't remember, but as a friend of Hilda I was got in to help and rode my bicycle all over London. In the evening when I got home and had put the bicycle away I went up to talk to Leonard[9] and Virginia, and drink cocoa; Bloomsbury was very addicted to cocoa. Virginia was fascinated to know what London was like on a bicycle. 'Did you go down Piccadilly? Were there hills? Did people shout at you?' She loved miscellaneous facts about other people's lives. Later, when I was qualified and had a job at University College Hospital, next door to Tavistock Square, I became interested in liver as a cure for pernicious anaemia, then a fatal disease. Medical research in those days was a rather primitive discipline. I went to the Professor of Medicine and said I would like to make some liver extract, which I had read about in the literature. He gave me some money to buy lots of liver, and an empty laboratory with necessary chemicals and glassware, and told me to go and borrow the mincing machines and pails of my friends. So of course I borrowed Virginia's mincing machine among others and her domestic pails and buckets and started work with a very inadequate account in some American journal to instruct me. This, again, fascinated Virginia. She followed all the details of my primitive chemical techniques, the fate of the dog on whom the extract was first tried, to see if it was safe, and then of the patient whom I cured. Finally, she wrote about it in *A Room of One's Own*. She used this activity of mine to illustrate how women have other interests besides what she called 'the perennial interests of domesticity'. 'Chloe liked Olivia. They shared a laboratory together ... these two young women were engaged in mincing liver, which is, it seems, a cure for pernicious anaemia'.[10]

This is one of the things I remember most clearly about Virginia, her endless interest in the details of other people's lives. If one went for a walk with her she would speculate about the people one met. 'Look, Janet, at that old woman – do you think she keeps a cat or a canary? Where do you think she is off to now? To visit a grandchild or to buy some new stockings?' And so it would go on.

Without words being spoken, I realized how closely she was involved in Leonard's work. I went upstairs for cocoa one night and found her packing. She explained to me 'Leonard is going up North tomorrow to some Labour Party meeting and, of course, as Leonard's wife, I must be there'. To me she was endlessly kind. When I went off to America for a year, I spent my last week-end with her and Leonard at Monk's House and, during my year away, she often wrote to me. The letters I fear were later lost in the London Blitz. When Madge Vaughan died she wrote 'I hope you won't mind me writing to you. I have thought so much of you since Madge's death. I can't described to you what she was like when she used to stay with us at St Ives and how we worshipped her'.

NOTES

Janet Maria Vaughan (1899–1993; DBE 1957), physician and medical researcher, specialising particularly in radiation problems and diseases of the blood. She was principal of Somerville College, Oxford from 1945 to 1967.

1. Woolf's parents: Leslie Stephen (1832–1904; knighted 1902), man of letters, biographer and first editor of the *Dictionary of National Biography*, and Julia, née Jackson (1846–95). John Addington Symonds (1840–93), writer on Renaissance Italy and on homosexuality, poet and autobiographer.
2. Margaret ('Madge') Vaughan, née Symonds (1869–1925). William Wyamar Vaughan (1865–1938), master of Wellington, later headmaster at Rugby College.
3. Cordelia Fisher, Woolf's cousin.
4. The hoax occurred on 10 February 1910 when the HMS *Dreadnought* was in Weymouth Bay. It occasioned questions in the House of Commons. See also p. 153.
5. The Sussex homes, respectively, of the Woolfs in Rodmell and of Vanessa Bell and Duncan Grant in nearby Charleston.

6. For information about Angelica Garnett, see p. 172.

7. Francis Frederick Locker Birrell (1889–1935), Garnett's business partner, journalist and drama critic. For information about David Garnett, see pp. 167–8. The Hogarth Press, established by Leonard and Virginia Woolf in 1917, moved from Richmond to 52 Tavistock Square in March 1924.

8. That is, in May 1926.

9. For information about Leonard Woolf, see p. 151.

10. *A Room of One's Own*, ch. V.

Meeting Virginia Woolf*

SIEGFRIED SASSOON

January 13 [1924] A quiet day, which ended noisily (most of the noise was made by myself talking about myself to Virginia and Leonard Woolf). I have wanted to meet V. W. since last April, when I read *Jacob's Room* at Garsington.[1] But I felt that the Woolfs belong to a rarefied intellectual atmosphere in which I should be ill at ease. I went to Paradise Road, Richmond, this evening, intending to be discreet and observantly detached. But the evening was a gossipy affair, very pleasant and unconstrained. V. W. drew me out adroitly, and I became garrulous. (Did I *bore* them once or twice?) Leonard Woolf seemed reticent and rather weary; anyhow my presence reduced him to comparative muteness. V. W. is a very fastidious lady, and looked lovely (in a lavender silk dress). She has very slender hands and a face for a miniature painter. We gossiped about the obvious names – Hardy, Gosse, Wells, Bennett, Lady Colefax, Middleton Murry, T. S. Eliot, Robert Graves, Aldous Huxley etc.[2] But the evening became more and more a monologue by me. I feel now as if I'd been 'showing-off', behaving like I used to do five years ago, when appearing at 'first meetings' with well-known authors. Talking in the self-explanatory style which one adopts (or indulges in) with new people who are sympathetic. Telling them about my 'commentative readings' in America, my family history, and so on. In fact, saying

* *Siegfried Sassoon Diaries 1923–1925*, ed. Rupert Hart-Davis (London: Faber and Faber, 1985) pp. 78–9.

things I've undoubtedly said before, with an air of producing them spontaneously. Perhaps my loquaciousness was only a symptom of shyness and anxiety to keep things going. Thank heaven, I avoided giving my 'war-experiences' turn. (Though I did touch on Craiglockhart Hospital, in connection with Wilfred Owen.[3]) They agreed with me about the modern vulgarisation of fine literature by the commercialism of publishers; and urged me to publish a book with the Hogarth Press. I dallied with the idea of a small volume of 'scraps of prose', vaguely visualising selections from my journal, which I feel now to be quite impracticable. We dined in their kitchen, which was pleasant and cosy. Ottoline told me that 'Virginia is very inhuman', but I found her charming.[4] But I am now wondering whether I can ever repeat my tour-de-force of 'creating a delightful impression'.

Talking about T. S. Eliot, V. W. said that the right way to treat him is to pull his leg, 'Old Tom' him, and so on; 'otherwise he behaves with such absurd formality and primness; he's rather an old prig, really, and needs to be chaffed out of it'. She also spoke of 'poor old Aldous', and evidently thinks his writings unimportant. This gratified me, as I'm getting fed up with being told that T. S. E. is the most important modern poet, and that Huxley is first-rate.

NOTES

Siegfried Loraine Sassoon (1886–1967), poet, biographer and diarist, known particularly for his poetry written during and after the First World War in which he served.

1. The country home of Lady Ottoline and Philip Morrell at Garsington, Oxfordshire, the site of lavish weekend parties attended by the artistic and literary avant-garde.
2. Thomas Hardy (1840–1928), novelist and poet; Sir Edmund Gosse (1849–1928), critic; H. G. Wells (1866–1946), short-story writer and novelist; Lady Sybil Colefax, society hostess; John Middleton Murry (1899–1957), critic and editor; Thomas Stearns Eliot (1888–1965), American-born poet and critic; Robert Graves (1885–1985), poet; Aldous Huxley (1894–1963), novelist. For information about Arnold Bennett, see p. 30.
3. Wilfred Owen (1893–1918), war poet. Sassoon encouraged Owen's work during the time Owen was invalided to Craiglockhart Hospital, Edinburgh.
4. For information about Lady Ottoline Morrell, see p. 28.

Mrs Woolf Comes to Dinner*

E. E. DUNCAN-JONES and U. K. N. STEVENSON

The visit of Miss Strachey's close friend, Virginia Woolf, in 1929 to read us a paper was a rather alarming occasion.[1] As I remember it she was nearly an hour late; and dinner in Clough Hall, never a repast for gourmets, suffered considerably. Mrs Woolf also disconcerted us by bringing a husband and so upsetting our seating plan. After the paper there was coffee with Mrs Woolf in the Principal's rooms. Mrs Woolf was really very well disposed to us as a group of intellectual young women; but we found her formidable. All I remember of her talk is that she praised very highly a poem of Stella Gibbons's, 'The Hippogriff'.[2] It was disquieting to learn later, when I was in Paris as a research student, that Mrs Woolf had brought out a book (*A Room of One's Own*) describing her Newnham dinner. Her purpose was, of course, to evoke pity for the poverty of the women's colleges: but at the time it made us, her hosts, decidedly uncomfortable.

* * *

I return once more to the room of my own. Because it was here, after, I think, the famous or infamous dinner, when prunes and custard were eaten and wine was not drunk, that Virginia Woolf stood and sat, and looked and spoke. She had come to address a Newnham society, and the post-address coffee and biscuits were distributed in my room, because it was a fairly large one. I think I had expected some profound, philosophic remarks, even after prunes and custard; but fixing me with that wonderful gaze, at once luminous and penetrating, what she actually said was, 'I'd no idea the young ladies of Newnham were so beautifully dressed'.

---

* From 'Mrs Woolf Comes to Dine' and 'A Room of One's Own', *A Newnham Anthology*, ed. Ann Philips (Cambridge: Cambridge University Press, 1979) pp. 174–5.

The prig in me was chagrined, even if my vanity sat up and purred; but over the years what has persisted has been the quality of her look, which seemed to say so much more than the words that came with it. The look held a hint of a smile, a hint of compassion, but it was above all an absolutely ruthless look; my pretty frock was no proof against it.

NOTES

1. Joan Pernel Strachey (1876–1951), Principal of Newnham College, Cambridge. Woolf addressed the Newnham Arts Society on 'Women & Fiction' on 20 October 1928.
2. Stella Dorothea Gibbons (1902–89), poet, novelist, journalist and short-story writer.

Virginia Woolf at Girton*

KATHLEEN RAINE

It was during the summer term that Virginia Woolf visited Girton – the first famous person with whom I had ever been in the same room. She came – it is all history now – at the invitation of the Girton Literary Society, to give her paper, A Room of One's Own.[1] The meeting took place in Girton's reception-room, with its mural panels, the work of a benefactor of the College who, having lived before the benefits of higher education, had devoted those long, idle Victorian hours (what happened to all that abundance of time after the turn of the century?) to embroidering in wool on ivory satin rather heavy foliage and flowers and birds and squirrels for the pleasure of those ladies who were to be educated away from the immemorial and symbolic occupations of Helen, Penelope, Persephone, and Blake's Daughters of Albion. The portrait of Lady Carew herself, in voluminous blue silk, hung over the chimney, reminding us that the eye of the Liberal aristocracy was upon all our comings and goings.[2] The grand piano, draped with a piece

* From The Land Unknown (London: Hamish Hamilton, 1975) pp. 21–3.

of oriental embroidery, was pushed to one side. Outside those tinted neo-Gothic windows cedar and tulip trees spread their branches over the sweep of the lawns upon whose green cedar-shaded carpet I was now no trespasser, but one of the happy and thrice-happy permitted to walk.

In the fairyland of the Girton reception-room, then, members of the Literary Society were gathered for coffee, after Hall; young Eton-cropped hair gleaming, Chinese shawls spread like the plumage of butterflies. (I vainly longed for one of those shawls, fringed with silk and embroidered with silken flowers and birds, fashionable at that time.) With Virginia Woolf had come her friend Victoria Sackville-West: the two most beautiful women I had ever seen.[3] I saw their beauty and their fame entirely removed from the context of what is usually called 'real' life, as if they had descended like goddesses from Olympus, to reascend when at the end of the evening they vanished from our sight. The divine *mana* may belong to certain beings merely by virtue of what they are; but *mana* belongs also to certain offices, royal or priestly; and masters in some art were, in those days, invested with the dignity of their profession. A 'great writer' had about him or about her an inherited glory shed from the greatness of writers of the past; and about Virginia Woolf this glory hovered. Every sacred office can be discredited, and in the present world, in England, the profession of the writer has been brought into disrepute by the same looting of sanctuaries as has taken place in other spheres of life.

I had not read any of Virginia Woolf's novels at the time; a few months before I had not even heard of her. Now from her famous paper I learned for the first time, and with surprise, that the problems of 'a woman writer' were supposed to be different from the problems of a man who writes; that the problem is not one of writing but of living in such a way as to be able to write. *A Room of One's Own* made claims on life far beyond mine: a room and a small unearned income were, to me, luxuries unimaginable. To elude the vigilance of my parents, and to write poems on the marble-topped table of a Lyons' or an ABC tea-shop was all I had at home, or for long after, hoped for. At Girton I had a room of my own; but while feeling it my due, I did not, at the same time, expect it to last, any more than a dream lasts; and yet, within that dream, we accept all that comes as a matter of course.

The pioneers to whom Girton owed its foundation had fought for the freedom I there enjoyed. Even so, I cannot truthfully say that I have ever found that my problems as a writer have been made greater or less by being a woman. The only problem – to write well and to write truly – is the same for either sex. As for time to write, there is always time. Volumes might have been written in the time of Lady Carew spent on all the wool embroidery upon satin. But perhaps the embroidery was a wiser choice, after all.

NOTES

Kathleen Jessie Raine (b. 1908), poet and autobiographer, counted among her Cambridge acquaintance William Empson, I. A. Richards and Bertrand Russell. Winner of the W. H. Smith award in 1972 for a book of poetry, she has also been Andrew Mellon Lecturer in Washington, DC.

1. Woolf went to Cambridge to address Girton College's ODTAA (One Damn Thing After Another) Society on 26 October 1928.
2. Julia (Mary), Lady Carew, née Lethbridge (d. 1922). In 1921 she donated to Girton College embroidered panels made by herself.
3. For information about Victoria ('Vita') Sackville-West, see p. 36.

Tea with Virginia Woolf*

G. E. EASDALE

September 15th, 1931. One of our great days! Mrs Virginia Woolf has been to tea.[1]

From the moment we woke up we have thought and prepared for nothing else.

The sun slowly but surely began to shine as the morning passed on, the sky to clear. Michael and Louise worked hard cleaning up the garden and helping me polish, dust and tidy the house. Every hour the September day became more charming, and the

* From *Middle Age, 1885–1932* (London: Constable, 1935) pp. 291–3.

house and garden; our excitement increased, we could think and talk of nothing else.

Then we sat and waited in the arbour.

At last we heard what we were sure was their car. It sounded quite different to any other car — 'That's it', we flew to the gate. And it began with the car getting fixed in the gate post, Mrs Woolf coming in by the kitchen garden, and our man-servant un-screwing the front bumper before Mr Woolf could drive in.

The gold-room was full of sunshine, with all its windows wide and the orchard seeming to crowd into the room. Mrs Woolf liked the honey sandwiches, lemon cake, the room being upstairs, the door to the attic and the everlasting flowers. How can I possibly describe her? I had expected to be acutely nervous, but I wasn't a bit. She was kind and gracious. Her hands are very fine and delicate, she glides, so that her feet scarcely seem to touch the ground. I wish I could write down everything she said, because everything she said was so well said. She has a delicious wit, it makes the commonest remark and incident sparkle. I must con-fess I was completely carried away by Mrs Woolf, swept as it were off my feet on a bright wave. I did not want to see, listen or speak to anyone else.

She wandered through the garden, lingered a moment by the orchard, pointed out the cyclamens in flower and then was gone like some swift ray of light travelling across a landscape changes familiar hedge and tree, field and hill into something rich and strange.

September 27th, 1931. Monk's House is a low long white house... enriched by chairs and tables decorated by Duncan Grant[2] and Vanessa Bell, and ripe apples lay about everywhere. Books abounded, and that for me gives distinction to a room: they lay on chairs, on tables and filled shelves. There were other guests, but somehow none of these people seemed to exist. From the moment we arrived, we were received with such kindness. It *was* I thought like entering another country, passing into Italy with its olive groves; this, I felt, is the kind of air my spirit loves.

Tea was set out on a long refectory table, with purple lustre ware, home-made bread and cakes, and honey from their hives. There were crumpets, too: these Mrs Woolf had specially bought to toast there and then herself, because it was her fancy, she said, to do so, as few, she continued, understood the pleasure of having crumpets for tea. The talk was richly embroidered by her humour and wit. In her entertaining way she described what happened when we wanted to illuminate our garden for Michael's twenty-first birthday party.

'A large party, you know, in their Kentish orchard. And their man-servant went out into their woods full of glow-worms to fill his large basket with two hundred; he came back with two'.

We wandered round the garden with Mr and Mrs Woolf. Leonard Woolf loves his flowers and tends his cyclamens in his glass-house with careful devotion. From the flowers we went into the old orchard where pear and apple trees were thick with fruit; at the end were the hives, and tall trees used as a rookery and the old wall of the churchyard.

'And here', Mrs Woolf said, 'is an old white owl that flies out over the mourners when there are funerals'.

She led us on to her green terrace where, she told us, she often walks; below it the plains stretched to the rising of the South Downs. Clumps of yellow dahlias edged the terrace, which was backed by a hedge of French honeysuckle. She took us to her writing-room, an out-door room with a great fig tree beside it. As we entered, I felt strangely moved. It was very light and had wide windows to the view she loved, of marshes and downs. Here, I thought, is the room of a great creative writer. Everything in this place about the house and garden, was eloquent. She took us to see the new room they had built; they have to come outside the house to get to it. Virginia Woolf likes to sleep there. Then we returned to the living-room and sat round the inglenook and talked of many things. Of ghosts and phantasms of the living, of poetry and accidents, of books and writers. Mrs Woolf excels as a talker and in making us all talk; with a touch here and there; she lights up with her own wit the plainest words.

At six we had to go, for we had over forty miles to travel, and there was that fear of what next would happen – after all, the car in several places was held together by safety-pins. They all came to see us off, and we returned safely through the dusk.

NOTES

Gladys Ellen Easdale, née Adeney (1885–19?), an amateur poet and a friend of the writer 'Mark Rutherford'.

1. For Woolf's description of this visit, on which Vita Sackville-West was to have accompanied her, see *Letters*, IV, 379.
2. For information about Duncan Grant, see p. 139.

Virginia*

ENID BAGNOLD

When I came to London at nineteen Bloomsbury was a kind of glittering village with no doors. It hovered ungeographically and had, to my mind, only one inhabitant – a woman with a magnet. I knew Lytton Strachey a little, and Desmond MacCarthy[1] very very well, but Virginia, at that time, I did not know.

Years and years went on. I was still an outsider, but not envious. Still Bloomsbury glittered fiercely, like something burning but not consumed. I might have tried to walk that way but I had turned slightly and walked into 'Society' – the camp which her brilliant nephew tells us Virginia only half despised.[2] Then the Woolfs came out of Bloomsbury into Sussex.

When I was riding I often saw Virginia striding; something red at her neck, or a red waistcoat. I waved but never stopped. So that it was odd and bold of me that when something funny happened to me and I stood alone in the hall of this house, smartly dressed and laughing and bursting to share it, I should cry out: 'The Woolfs!'

What had happened was that someone who thought he knew me and didn't, who thought I was a Member but I wasn't, had telephoned to ask me to go racing at Goodwood with him and had had to pay for my Entry and my champagne luncheon. Asked so suddenly I had no money with me. I could have written a

* *Adam International Review*, no. 364–6 (1972) p. 15.

cheque but I forgot I could. Then my hat had blown across the horses at the Start and all Scatter Wilson's bets went wrong.

I was laughing too much in the hall to put up with it. I rang the Woolfs – they said come – I was at Rodmell in twenty minutes. I was fearless. I told it so that we adored it together. It was the other-worldish disaster that they loved. The sense of Scatter's dismay. How he said with horror to the Duke of Richmond: 'I won't have to pay for her, will I?' And the Duke's immovable, 'Yes, you will'. 'And the drive back?' said Leonard. 'In silence. We never spoke a word'.

Virginia leant, listening magically, her face on her hand, laughing. Leonard, his hand trembling on the way to his mouth with a scone, egged me on, picking over the disaster, finding new bits, looking for more. I dined later with Leonard and Virginia, and, much nearer the end, lunched with Virginia and Vita. Virginia wrote in her *Writer's Diary*: 'Now to write, with a new nib, to Enid Jones'. And a week later: '...tomorrow Vita; then Enid'.[3] It was at that lunch that Virginia strangely asked me if I had any Dexadrine. But I had none. Then she died. Snatched away. Was it going to have been friendship – after all those years?

Rottingdean, November 1972

NOTES

Enid Algerine Bagnold, Lady Jones (1889–1981), journalist, novelist and playwright, best known for her novel *National Velvet* (1935).

1. Giles Lytton Strachey (1880–1932), biographer and essayist. Charles Otto Desmond MacCarthy (1877–1952; knighted 1951), critic and literary editor. Both were members of the Bloomsbury Group.
2. Quentin Bell (b. 1910), artist, art critic and professor of art, author of *Virginia Woolf: A Biography* (1972).
3. Entries for 26 January and 16 February 1941, *Diary*, v, 355, 356.

Part II
Moments of Being

The Diary of Sydney Waterlow*

Th. 8. [December 1910] Dined with the Clive Bells; what a relief & change![1] No one else but Virginia S. We had talk that begins to be really intimate. Vanessa very amusing on paederasty among their circle. I realised for the first time the difference between her & Virginia: Vanessa icy, cynical, artistic; Virginia much more emotional, & interested in life rather than beauty. A glorious evening.

Tu. 15. [August 1911, Cambridge] Tea with R. Brooke:[2] Virginia Stephen there.

Sun. 10. [March 1912] Lunched with H. James at the Reform . . .[3] Asked much after Virginia & Vanessa: can't cultivate Gordon Sq. because of the unpleasant presence of 'that little image' Clive. 'Tell Virginia – tell her – how sorry I am that the inevitabilities of life shd have made it seem possible even for a moment that I would allow any child of her father's to swim out of my ken'.

[August 1912: Pasted clipping from a newspaper:] WOOLF: STEPHEN. – On Saturday, the 10th Aug., at the St Pancras Register Office, LEONARD SIDNEY WOOLF, son of the late Sidney Woolf, Q.C., and of Mrs Sidney Woolf, of Lexham, Colinette-road, Putney, to VIRGINIA STEPHEN, daughter of the late Sir Leslie Stephen, K.C.B.

NOTES

Sydney Philip Perigal Waterlow (1878–1944; knighted 1935), career civil servant in the Foreign Office. Waterlow read classics at Trinity College, Cambridge, and came to Bloomsbury as a friend of Thoby Stephen. He proposed to Virginia Woolf in 1911.

* Not previously published. From the diaries of Sydney Waterlow, Berg Collection, New York Public Library.

1. Bell had recently been helping Hilton Young, who was electioneering.
2. Rupert Chawner Brooke (1887–1915), poet, remembered especially for his poems written during the war.
3. Henry James (1843–1916), distinguished American-born novelist and short-story writer, a friend of Leslie Stephen.

At the Theatre*

BERTA RUCK

Lydia, however (invariably one to speak her mind in her enchantingly original English) said, 'This is so doll'.

'Lydia! It's *not* dull. It's very funny, very *funny*'.

'It is doll. We will go out'.

'We can't', said your Aunt in a whisper, 'At least wait until the Interval'.

'We will go out now. It is too doll to bear. Now. Come'.

'We can't, possibly —'

'No one will see'.

'Lydia, *everybody* will see us! We are all much to noticeable —

We were you know. Your famous Aunt wore a very large black sombrero hat, I was as tall as she, and had fat black plaits done over my ears, Lydia between us was small, but always outstandingly striking in movement and manner, you might not see what she wore, but she drew every eye.

Fortunately she allowed herself to be persuaded to sit down and see it out before the audience joined in!

* From a letter to Quentin Bell, 11 September 1971, about a performance of Euripides' *Helen* and *Cyclops* by the Cambridge Amateur Dramatic Company at the Chiswick Empire on 9 May 1925 to which Lydia Lopokova[1] had invited Berta Ruck and Virginia Woolf.

NOTE

Amy Roberta Ruck (1878–1978), novelist and writer of radio scripts. Born in British India, she studied art at the Slade School and in Paris but devoted her career (1914–72) to writing popular fiction.

1. Lydia Vasilievna Lopokova (1892–1981), ballerina in Diaghilev's Ballets Russes and later wife of the economist John Maynard Keynes. For Woolf's comments on the occasion, see entry for 9 May 1925, *Diary*, III, 17.

The Diary of Lady Ottoline Morrell*

May 1917 [London] Virginia Woolf came to tea with me. She entered with such energy and vitality and seemed to me far the most imaginative and masterly intellect that I had met for many years. She played on life with her imagination as a Paderewski plays on the piano.[1] I was dazzled by her.

[*November*] *1917* [Garsington] Virginia and Leonard Woolf have been here for the week-end.[2] I thought her extraordinarily beautiful and supremely eminent. Her generalizations and her swiftness of mind astounded me. She sat as if on a throne and took it for granted that we must worship. She seemed to feel certain of her own eminence. It is true, but it is rather crushing, for I feel she is very contemptuous of other people. When I stretched out a hand to feel another woman, I found only a very lovely, clear intellect. She does not seem to realize human beings as they are, but has a fantastic vision of them as strange birds or fishes living in air or water in an unreal world. They always seem transposed. She and Lytton who was here at the same time seemed like complementary intellects, but he is more rational and real, and she has more vigour and imagination. She seems to come at full sail up to a

* From *Ottoline at Garsington: Memoirs of Lady Ottoline Morrell 1915–1918*, ed. Robert Gathorne-Hardy (London: Faber and Faber; New York: Knopf, 1975) pp. 179, 244–5.

subject one expects her to tackle and to combat and conquer the problem, but generally she evades the crucial moment: I suppose if one has very little real knowledge of human beings or of the forces of life it is almost impossible to solve human problems; they always remain without a start or a finish, suspended between earth and heaven above.

When we were talking about keeping a journal, I said mine was filled with thoughts and struggles of my inner life. She opened her eyes wide in astonishment. Her eyes are like falcon's eyes and express so little. But she seems in some odd way more united than most of us, as if she never worried or troubled about anyone. She talked of her book *Night and Day*. The theme of it is that we all live in some dream world of our own with occasional rocks of real life emerging, but the dream is the ether round us. I think that is her feeling about the world and one sees that her dream is far more fanciful and often more beautiful than that of most people, which makes her very remote from our dreams. Again and again, I felt she was like a great bird sailing by, that alights to parley for a few moments and then resumes her flight. As long as she can live in her dream I think she is happy, but I believe at times she realizes her isolation and that life presents an insoluble problem to her. She flies above the earth but has no contact with heaven.

[1936] These were my impressions of Virginia in 1917 and they seem to me . . . to have been true of her then. But as years have passed I have been able to get into closer touch with her and have found her a very enchanting faithful friend. Her intellect is so highly sensitive, so subtle that it lights up the world to her with a more brilliant light than to most of us. How ruthless she can be! But how much I love her!

NOTES

Lady Ottoline Violet Anne Morrell, née Cavendish-Bentinck (1873–1938), celebrated hostess and patron of the arts whose London and Oxfordshire homes served as salons for the literary and artistic avant-garde. Particularly connected with Bertrand Russell (whose mistress she briefly was) and D. H. Lawrence, she also moved on Bloomsbury's fringes.

1. Ignace Jan Paderewski (1860–1941), Polish pianist, composer and statesman.
2. The Woolfs spent 17–19 November 1917 at Garsington. See *Diary*, I, 77–9.

Mr Bennett and Mrs Woolf*

ARNOLD BENNETT

November 4th [1926] We were ten minutes late for dinner at H. G. Wells's,[1] and H. G. himself was eleven minutes late. The Shaws[2] were there, and Frank Wells, and Marjorie Craig (H. G.'s morning secretary) and the Leonard Woolfs. Both gloomy, these two last. But I liked both of them in spite of their naughty treatment of me in the press.[3] Shaw talked practically the whole time, which is the same thing as saying that he talked a damn sight too much. After dinner he and Dorothy and Virginia Woolf and H. G. formed a group and never moved. I formed another group with Charlotte Shaw and Jane Wells,[4] and never moved either. I really wanted to have a scrap with Virginia Woolf; but got no chance.

13 December 1925: To Harriet Cohen My child, I reck little of V. Woolf. This is putting it mildly. I have had trouble with Dorothy over this authoress. But Swinnerton[5] & I *know* we are right about her...

1 December 1930: To Richard Bennett Last night I was at Ethel Sands'[6] and had a great pow-wow with Virginia Woolf. (Other guests held their breath to listen to us.) Virginia is all right.

* From *The Journal of Arnold Bennett 1921–1928*, ed. Newman Flower (London: Cassell; New York: Viking, 1933) p. 188 and *Letters of Arnold Bennett*, vol. III: *1916–1931*, ed. James Hepburn (London: Oxford University Press, 1970) pp. 256, 257n.

NOTES

Enoch Arnold Bennett (1867–1931), novelist and prolific journalist. His *The Old Wives' Tale* (1908) and *Clayhanger Trilogy* (1910–15) brought him widespread popularity.

1. Herbert George Wells (1866–1946), novelist and short-story writer.
2. George Bernard Shaw (1856–1950), dramatist and essayist.
3. Virginia Woolf's famous essay 'Mr Bennett and Mrs Brown' (1924) attacks Bennett's methods and attitudes towards fiction.
4. Jane Wells, née Amy Catherine Robbins (1872–1927), Wells's second wife. Charlotte Frances Shaw, née Payne-Townshend (d. 1943).
5. Frank Arthur Swinnerton (1884–1982), novelist, reviewer and publisher's reader.
6. Ethel Sands (1873–1962), American-born painter, moving in literary circles.

The Diary of Beatrice Webb*

BEATRICE WEBB

6 February 1927 [Passfield Corner]   The Leonard Woolfs spent the week-end here – we had lost sight of them and were glad to renew relations with this exceptionally gifted pair.[1] A dozen years ago, when we first saw them, they were living under a cloud – she on the borderline of lunacy, he struggling desperately to keep her out of a mental home. For some years it seemed doubtful whether he would succeed. Now the cloud has passed away. Her appearance has altered: instead of a beautiful but loosely knit young woman, constantly flushing and with a queer, uncertain, almost hysterical manner, she is, though still beautiful, a spare, self-contained ascetic-looking creature, startlingly like her father, Leslie Stephen; the same tall, stooping figure, exquisite profile; refined, an almost narrow and hard intellectuality of expression. Woolf also is matured and has lost his nervous shyness. Wholly

* From *The Diary of Beatrice Webb*, vol. 4: *1924–1943: 'The Wheel of Life'*, ed. Norman and Jeanne Mackenzie (London: Virago; Cambridge, Mass.: Harvard University Press, 1985) pp. 112–13, 443–4, 466–7.

unconventional in their outlook on life and manners, belonging rather to a decadent set (Clive Bell is her brother-in-law) but themselves puritanical, they are singularly attractive to talk to. In one matter they are not up-to-date, for they are rigid secularists, regarding theology or even mysticism as *l'infâme*.[2] Here his Jewish blood comes in: he quite clearly is revolted by the Christian myth, the anger of a Jew at an apostate from the Judaic faith. (Considering the persecution of the Jews right up to the nineteenth century by the Christian Church, I wonder why they are not more obsessed by hatred of the author of Christianity.) He is an anti-imperialist fanatic but otherwise a moderate in Labour politics – always an opponent of 'workers' control' and 'proletarianism'. She is uninterested in politics – wholly literary – an accomplished critic of style and a clever artist in personal psychology, disliking the 'environmental' novel of late Victorian times, especially its latest exponent, Arnold Bennett. Like other works of the new school of novelists, I do not find her work interesting outside its craftsmanship, which is excellent but *précieuse*. Her men and women do not interest me – they don't seem worth describing in such detail; the mental climate in which they live seems strangely lacking in light, heat, visibility and variety; it is a dank mist of insignificant and monotonous thoughts and feelings, no predominant aims, no powerful reactions from their mental environment, a curious impression of automatic existence when one state of mind follows another without any particular reason. To the aged Victorian this soullessness is depressing. Doubtless our insistence on a purpose, whether for the individual or the universe, appears to them a delusion and a pernicious delusion.

The last hours with them were spent in a raging argument about denominational education and the validity of religious mysticism. They were against toleration. What was 'manifestly false' was *not* to be taught at the public expense and not to be *thought* by persons above a certain level of intelligence who claimed to be honest with themselves and other people. I pleaded for 'the endowment of error', and threatened them with fundamentalism, or Roman Catholicism, if they insisted on universal and compulsory sectarianism.

27 October 1940 [Passfield Corner]   I journeyed up to London in a train crowded with officers in uniform and youths looking sad and distraught, saying farewell to mothers and sweethearts, and a few older men to wives and children at the stations – to lunch with Barbara[3] and meet the Leonard Woolfs. They had expressed a desire to meet me again. Leonard was looking terribly ill with his trembling hands, but was as gently wise as ever. . . .

Virginia seemed troubled by an absence of any creed as to what was right and what was wrong. I asked her whether she was going to write a second volume of *The Years*. I longed to hear how the family she described so vividly would respond to this new war. Would they be as unconcerned as they were during the great war of 1914–18? She gave me no answer except that she did not know her own mind about what was happening – so how could she describe the mind of others! ... This gifted and charming lady, with her classic features, subtle observation and symphonic style, badly needs a living philosophy. Brought up in the innermost circle of the late Victorian intellectuals, in revolt against the Christian religion with its superstitions and its hypocritical conventions, they were between *laissez-faire* and *laissez-aller* in all the circumstances of life. *Absence of restraint* was to them the one and only meaning of liberty, for they personally enjoyed the presence of opportunity to lead the life they liked, or thought they liked. Virginia Woolf realizes that this creed has broken down; but she sees no way out... We all aim at maximizing human happiness, health, loving kindness, scientific certainty and the spirit of adventure together with the appreciation of beauty in sight and sound, in word and thought. Where we differ is how to bring about this ideal here and now.

7 April 1941 [Passfield Corner]   In the morning news: 'Mrs Virginia Woolf, missing from her home since Friday 28th ... assumed drowned in the river Ouse'. During the day and for some days afterwards, ghosts from the past haunted me – that tall, talented woman with her classic features, her father Leslie Stephen, also tall, good-looking, highly cultured, with whom in the 80s I used to discuss English history in the house of Alice Green in Kensington Square.[4] An old man, seemingly kind and courteous to a young writer but pictured as a supreme egotist towards his family by his daughter with a bitter pen in *To the Lighthouse*, perhaps her most successful novel.

Virginia was a beautiful woman and a writer of great charm and finesse – in her *uniqueness* the most outstanding of our women novelists. The Woolfs stayed with the Webbs, and the Webbs with

the Woolfs, and Leonard was one of Sidney's most intimate col-
leagues in international propaganda during the great war; but
we never became sympathetic friends. I think we liked them better
than they liked us. In a way which I never understood, I offended
Virginia. I had none of her sensitiveness, her understanding of
the inner life of the subjective man, expressed in the birth, life
and death of social institutions. Also we clashed with Leonard
Woolf in our conception of what constitutes human freedom: the
absence of restraint for the intellectual or the presence of opportunity for the ordinary man – which element was to be the foremost
object of the social reformer? In particular, he abhorred Soviet
Communism. But in spite of this mental aloofness from the Woolfs
I am pained by the thought of that beautiful and brilliant Virginia
yielding to the passion for death rather than endure the misery of
continued life. Twenty years ago her devoted husband had nursed
her through a period of mental derangement and suicidal mania.
In middle age she became a vigorous and a seemingly self-assured
woman, an eminently successful author and a devoted companion
to her distinguished husband. What led to the tragedy? And what
is happening to the ultra-refined, public-spirited and gifted Leonard
Woolf? The last time I saw them both was at a luncheon at Barbara's
about eighteen months ago. Her last words to me, as she and
Leonard met, were 'I have no living philosophy' – which may probably account for her voluntary withdrawal from life.

NOTES

Martha Beatrice Webb, née Potter (1858–1943), social activist, devoted
her life to the Fabian cause, investigating and exposing social injustices
in books, pamphlets and lectures. With her husband Sydney (1859–1947),
she established the London School of Economics and founded the *New
Statesman*.

1. See entry for 29 January 1927, *Diary*, III, 126, for Woolf's account
of this visit.
2. After Voltaire's famous saying about the Roman Catholic Church:
'*Ecrasez l'infâme*' (Crush the infamy).
3. Barbara Drake (1876–1963), Webb's favourite niece.
4. Alice Sophia Amelia Green (1847–1929), historian and literary and
political hostess.

A Week in France with Virginia Woolf*

VITA SACKVILLE-WEST

Monday Sept 24. 1928. I went by train to Lewes where Virginia and Leonard met me. We drove to Rodmell where I saw Pinker's puppies.[1] Leonard then motored us to Newhaven where we caught the 11.30 boat. We took our lunch with us and ate it on board. It was very calm. We arrived at Dieppe at 3. and took the train to Paris. In Paris we went to the Hotel de Londres, rue Bonaparte. We left our luggage & walked out to have dinner in a small restaurant on B^d. Raspail. Walking out we got into a bookshop where V. bought *J'adore* by Jean Desbordes, & I bought *L'Immoraliste*.[2] There was an old man sitting in the bookshop, & he & the proprietor (a woman) fired off a rhapsody about Proust. We observed how this could never happen in England, – it was about 8 o'clock, yet there was the old customer sitting & discussing Proust, also Desbordes of whose literary success he said Cocteau[3] would soon be jealous, 'even if he had no other causes for jealousy'.

Walking home from the restaurant we missed our way, so sat down to drink coffee at the brasserie Lutetia in rue de Sèvres – & V. & I wrote to Leonard and Harold respectively on the torn-out fly-leaves of our books.[4] She told me how she & Leonard had had a small & sudden row that morning about her going abroad with me.

A rather disturbed night, as fire-engines tore down the street beneath my window.

Tuesday 25th. Called at 6 – & drove to the Gare de Lyon through a deserted Paris. Caught the 7 o'clock train to Saulieu where we arrived at 12.40. I read *L'Immoraliste*. V. read *J'adore*, & remarked that there was a tendency in young Frenchmen of today towards

---

* Not previously published. Berg Collection, New York Public Library.

religion and simplicity. Hotel de la Poste at Saulieu, with excellent cooking. After lunch we went out; a fair in progress; V. bought a green corduroy coat for Leonard. We then went & sat in a field till it got too cold, & wrote letters. After dinner we went to the fair. There was a zoo with lion-cubs, a merry-go round, & a Bal Tabarin which we watched for some time. A very lovely gipsy woman there. Virginia very much delighted with all these sights. People threw confetti over us.

Wednesday 26th. We had breakfast in my room, and entered on a heated argument about men & women. V. is curiously feminist. She dislikes the possessiveness and love of domination in men. In fact she dislikes the quality of masculinity. Says that women stimulate her imagination, by their grace & their art of life. We then went out & I bought myself a corduroy coat. After lunch we went for quite a long walk, past the station & down the lanes between the woods. Nice, but not warm enough. After dinner V. read me her memoir of 'Old Bloomsbury',[5] and we talked a lot about her brother.

Thursday 27th. We left Saulieu at 8. and got to Avallon at 9.30. Here we walked about looking at the town; church of St Lazare, old houses, ramparts, etc – with a fine view over the valley. I got letters from H. at the poste restante. V. was very much upset because she heard nothing from Leonard. We lunched at Hotel de la Poste where we fell in with Valerie motoring to Avignon with the John Balderstons.[6] We went again to the post; still nothing from Leonard; so I made V. send a telegram.[7] We hired a motor & drove to Vézelay which enchants us. Went out to look at the cathedral, and view from the terrace; then lay in a field not talking much, but just listening to the crickets. V. seemed tired, & I made her go to bed at 1/4 to 10. In the middle of the night I was woken up by a thunderstorm. Went along to V's room thinking she might be frightened. We talked about science & religion for an hour – and the ultimate principle – and then as the storm had gone over I left her to go to sleep again.

Friday 28th. A rainy morning. We sat in my room & wrote letters. At 11. it cleared up & we went out, to the antiquaire where we bought nothing. Fitful sunshine, & I took some photographs. After lunch we walked down to Asquins, & sat for some time in a vineyard & again on the banks of the Cure – where we watched the old village women doing the washing. Then up the hill, with lovely views down over the valley of the Cure. I made V. go in and rest, and walked right round the ramparts myself looking at the sunset.

Saturday 29ᵗʰ.   Left Vézelay with great regret at 10. A lovely warm morning. I watched the builders on their ladders handing up the stones. Motored to Sermizelles, & there caught a train at 10.49 which got us to Auxerre for lunch. Hotel Touring. A thunderstorm burst, so we waited; then went out & found lovely stained glass in St Etienne. Went to St Gervais where there is an old crypt, – not very interesting. Nice bridges over the river. Had chocolate in a tea-shop & found a good antiquaire where V. bought a looking-glass. Discussed Edith Sitwell. V. told me the history of her early loves, – Madge Symon[d]s, who is Sally in *Mrs Dalloway*.

Sunday 30ᵗʰ.   Got up at 6. & left for Paris at 7. Drove from Gare de Lyon to St Lazare, where we lunched & then went to Rouen.[8]

NOTES

Victoria Mary ('Vita') Sackville-West (1892–1962), novelist, poet and gardener, the model for *Orlando*. In addition to her literary writing, she also wrote extensively about travel and gardening.

1. Pinker (or Pinka), the Woolfs' dog, the model for the protagonist of *Flush*.
2. Jean Cocteau (1889–1963), playwright and poet.
3. Published in 1928, the first novel by Jean Desbordes (1906–44). André Gide's *L'Immoraliste* was published in 1902.
4. Letter of [24 September 1928], *Letters*, III, 533–4.
5. See *Moments of Being: Unpublished Autobiographical Writings of Virginia Woolf*, ed. Jeanne Schulkind (Brighton: Sussex University Press, 1976).
6. Valerie Taylor, an actress. John Balderston (1889–1954), American playwright and writer of screen plays, then London correspondent for the *New York World*.
7. See telegram to Leonard Woolf, 27 September 1928, *Letters*, III, 538.
8. Woolf and Sackville-West returned to England on 1 October. Woolf wrote her husband daily letters during this sojourn (*Letters*, III, 534–9).

At Elizabeth Bowen's*

CYRIL CONNOLLY

[April 1934]   Ireland quite derelict, empty and down at heel. Elizabeth [Bowen]'s house[1] lovely but rather forlorn. The country so cold, as usual. Owing to rural torpor increased by the relaxing climate all literary effort is here impossible so will only summarise briefly. Next day (Sat) go to have tea at Anne's grave. Woolfs arrive. He small spare intellectual Jew, she lovely, shy and virginal. They seem shocked by Jean's[2] dress (Virginia asked Elizabeth what unnatural vice was) and talked only of plans and motoring. Occasional flickers of animation over the boringness of Arthur Waley and Bob Trevelyan, and the difficulty of entertaining (why should drink be necessary?).[3] Virginia Woolf gave a satirical description of G. B. Stern.[4] We agreed that we could not like people if we didn't like their books. They left next morning.[5]

NOTES

Cyril Vernon Connolly (1903–74), reviewer and essayist. A prolific and influential commentator on literary trends, Connolly co-founded *Horizon* (1940–50), the leading periodical of its day.

1. For information about Elizabeth Bowen, see p. 172. Bowen's Court is the subject of a memoir by Bowen published in 1942.
2. Jean Connolly, his wife.
3. Arthur David Waley (1889–1966), poet and translator, an authority on Japanese and Chinese literature. Robert Caverley Trevelyan (1872–1951), classics scholar and poet, elder brother of the historian G. M. Trevelyan.
4. Gladys Bertha Stern (1890–1973), prolific popular novelist.
5. For Woolf's impressions of this encounter, see entry for 3 February 1927, *Diary*, IV, 210, and a letter to Vanessa Bell, *Letters*, V, 229.

* From *Journal and Memoir*, ed. David Pryce-Jones (London: Collins, 1983; New York: Ticknor & Fields, 1984) pp. 254–5.

'She enjoyed each butterfly aspect of the world'*

DAME EDITH SITWELL

Virginia Woolf had a moonlit transparent beauty. She was exquisitely carved, with large thoughtful eyes that held no foreshadowing of that tragic end which was a grief to everyone who had ever known her. To be in her company was delightful. She enjoyed each butterfly aspect of the world and of the moment, and would chase the lovely creatures, but without damaging the coloured dust on their wings. Whenever anyone present said anything pregnant, she would clasp her long delicate hands together and laugh with pleasure. In her own talk she always went straight to the point.

For instance, on the first occasion when I met her, at a dinner party given by Osbert and Sacheverell,[1] she asked me, 'Why do you live where you do?'

'Because I have not much money'.

'How much money a year have you?'

I told her.

'Oh well, I think we can do better for you than that', she said thoughtfully.

However, nothing came of this project, and I remained in Bayswater.

That, I think, was as well. I do not think I should have 'fitted into' the closely serried company of Bloomsbury. I was not an unfriendly young woman, but I was shy, and yet, at unexpected moments, was not silent – and silence was much prized, sometimes to the embarrassment of persons outside the inner circle of Bloomsbury.

---

* From *Taken Care Of: An Autobiography* (London: Hutchinson; New York: Atheneum, 1965) pp. 93–4.

NOTES

Edith Louise Sitwell (1887–1964), poet particularly noted for her unconventional style and for her poetry written during the Second World War. Her prose work includes a study of Pope and *English Eccentrics* (1933). Highly original, she dressed theatrically and possessed a striking manner.

1. Sitwell's brothers, also writers. For information about Sir Osbert Sitwell, see p. 52. Sir Sacheverell Sitwell (1897–1988), poet, biographer and writer on art and travel.

The Diary of Dame Ethel Smyth*

[1933] I don't think I have ever cared for anyone more profoundly, and it is I think because of her genius. One can't have relations with her as with others. The fact is you have to take what you can get of Virginia.

I learned to know her too late, when my deafness was increasing. I mind that most because of her and music.

I met her first three years ago in 1930 and for 18 months I really thought of little else. I think this proves what I have always held – that for many women, anyhow for me, passion is independent of the sex machine. Of course when you are young, it will not be gainsaid. (Nor indeed if I am frank, did it cease to play any part with men when I should have done with all things physical.... But I have remained capable of a love as deep and absorbing as one or two major loves of my youth.)

Of course there are two great factors – her genius and her beauty. Also her most wonderful speaking voice, and a distinction and a fascination which no words can describe. But the odd thing is her loveableness.

I think she has very grave faults. Absolutely self-absorbed and (no wonder), jealous of literary excellence; (couldn't see the point

* From Christopher St John, *Ethel Smyth: A Biography* (London: Longmans, Green, 1959) pp. 222–4.

of D. H. Lawrence until he was dead).[1] Ungenerous, indeed incapable of knowing what generosity means, I had almost said,
but she recognizes it in others. In Vita, for instance, who I think
is the only person except Vanessa Bell (her sister) and Leonard,
her husband, whom she really loves.

She is arrogant, intellectually, beyond words yet absolutely
humble about her own great gift. Her integrity fascinates me. To
save your life, or her own, she could not doctor what she thinks
to be the truth.

Of religion she has no conception. Her views, and the views of
all that Bloomsbury group, about it are quite childish. Also their
political views. They think all aristocrats are limited and stupid,
and swallow all the humbugging shibboleths of the Labour Party.

How far V. is human I don't know. She is very incalculable,
and has never been known to admit that she can be in the wrong.
And yet you love her, love her.

I have had two or three rows with her for odd reasons. Do I
say *reasons*? Why I have never known what it was about! She is
utterly unforgiving then, and you just have to wait until the storm
dies down.

At one time, having knocked herself to pieces in life, she went
mad, and twice tried to kill herself. But Leonard and Vanessa
coaxed her back to sanity. And then began this output of genius
which has not yet reached its zenith.... I can't get on with *The
Waves*, and I rather doubt the judgment of those, mainly quite
young people, who rave about it. But her second volume of *The
Common Reader* is superb.

Much in her – especially the clash of adoring solitude and also
adoring smart parties, and the clash of hating 'words, words' with
a love of talk – puzzles me.

She is the most marvellous letter-writer and likes me to write
to her which she says is as easy to me as rolling marbles down a
board. And after 2 or 3 times to her, I get, in her exquisite hand-
writing a letter from her, as clearly cut, as absolutely devoid of
one unnecessary word as speech can be, and often funny with a
wit only V. has.

She is very vain, and tried not to be, but can't help it. If she heard that someone thought her books very overrated, she wouldn't care at all. But if she heard these snooks had said her eyes were too close together (which they are perhaps) she would be thoroughly annoyed.

What is amusing is her loving to cut a dash – to put on a smart gown and go to a function, and then despising herself for it.

I think she is fond of me in her odd reserved way.... She came to stay with me one night last year and says she is coming again almost immediately. It seems too good to be true, and it is not easy for her, yet I daresay she will. I have lots of nice names for her. '4d. for 9d.' because she asks a lot, and gives little – in *quantity* at least. Never wants to see one more than about once a month. '*Frozen falcon*' – someone who sat behind her at a concert said she looked like that – so still, so alert.

When she comes into a room it is as if one from another world entered. Her distinction? So exquisitely delicate, yet such a sense of strength.... The only thing she can't do well is ... laugh. *Le rire fidèle* is not her line, and that's odd for there is occasionally a very hilarious strain in her work, and as for her letters! Ah!!

She bulked too large in my life for sanity when I thought I could have an ordinary friendship with her, and hoped on. Now I know you can't, and have got her just rightly placed in my life.... I have learned to conquer the feeling. 'I've got so little pudding I can't eat it'.

She's a very good starter. At the beginning of all things I was asked to Monk's House (their cottage at Rodmell) for the night, but it will never happen again. It's not their way, and I so utterly feel this that I don't even want it to.... That is the wonderful thing about her. You don't think therefore she likes you less, nor ask consistency of her. But oh! I wish I had a car and could sometimes bear her down here for a night. Only I don't think Leonard would be resigned to her not being there always, always. Besides which Virginia is happiest leading a daily round, common task life, and he knows it. (Damn them both.)

I have masses more to say about her, and this is a miserable effort. But as I am now going to keep my diary as heretofore, she will come into it. I had to sort of get her off my chest before I could begin the new epoch. Only this I must say. I don't believe anyone as big as she is can help wishing to get nicer to me. When we have had rows, it has generally been because she considered something I had said implied a low estimate of her – morally or somehow. I have rejoined: 'Has one no credit at your bank? Given what you know of my devotion to you, does it never occur to you, I *can't* have meant it that way?' Only her passion of fury – the slightly insane streak in her on which I am convinced her terrific gift depends – has to expend itself. She can be cruel then, and may say something that lashes one across the face, but she has to give that flick. Fortunately in the new epoch the flick no longer hurts.

NOTES

Ethel Mary Smyth (1858–1944; DBE 1922), composer, autobiographer and feminist. After studying music in Leipzig, where she became associated with Brahms's circle, Smyth pursued a career that in addition to small-scale works included the composition of operas and oratorios.

1. David Herbert Lawrence (1885–1930), novelist, poet and critic.

Part III
Among Friends

Virginia in Spain*

GERALD BRENAN

It was in the spring of 1923 that Leonard and Virginia Woolf
came out to see me. I met them at Granada at the house of some
friends of mine, the Temples, who wished to discuss the African
colonies with Leonard, and after a couple of nights there we came
on by bus and mule to Yegen. This time the journey went smoothly,
without any of the difficulties that had marked Lytton Strachey's
passage three years before, and it was evident that they enjoyed it.

The first thing that comes to my mind when I think of Virginia
as she was in those days, and particularly as I saw her in the
quiet seclusion of my house, is her beauty. Although her face
was too long for symmetry, its bones were thin and delicately
made and her eyes were large, grey or greyish blue, and as clear
as a hawk's. In conversation they would light up a little coldly
while her mouth took an ironic and challenging fold, but in re-
pose her expression was pensive and almost girlish. When in the
evening we settled under the hooded chimney and the logs burned
up and she stretched out her hands to the blaze, the whole cast
of her face revealed her as a poet.

There are writers whose personality resembles their work, and
there are others who, when one meets them, give no inkling of
it. Virginia Woolf belonged strikingly to the first category. When
one had spent half an hour in a room with her one could easily
believe that it was she who, as one was told, had scribbled quickly
in purple ink in the summer house at Rodmell that fresh and
sparkling article that had just appeared in *The Nation*, and when
one saw her in a reflective or dreamy mood one recognized only
a little less slowly the authoress of *To the Lighthouse*. One reason
for this was that her conversation, especially when she had been
primed up a little, was like her prose. She talked as she wrote

* From *South from Granada* (London: Hamish Hamilton; New York: Farrar,
Straus and Cudahy, 1957) pp. 139–42 and *Personal Record: 1920–1972* (London:
Jonathan Cape, 1974; New York: Knopf, 1975) p. 58.

45

and very nearly as well, and that is why I cannot read a page of
The Common Reader today without her voice and intonation coming back to me forcibly. No writer that I know of has put his
living presence into his books to the extent that she has done.

Not, however, that what she said was ever bookish. She talked
easily and naturally in a pure and idiomatic English, often, like
many of her friends, in a lightly ironical tone. Irony, it will be
remembered plays a great and important part in her writings.
There it is of a gay and playful kind, sometimes verging on face-
tiousness, but in her conversation it became personal and took
on a feminine, and one might almost say flirtatious, form. Leaning sideways and a little stiffly in her chair she would address
her companion in a bantering tone, and she liked to be answered
in the same manner. But whatever her vein, all the resources of
her mind seemed to be at her immediate disposal at every moment.
One felt a glass-like clarity, but it was not the clarity of a logician,
but rather that of a kaleidoscope which throws out each time from
the same set of pieces a different pattern. Much later, when she
was, I think, working on *The Waves*, she told me that her difficulty lay in stopping the flow of her pen. She had been reading,
she said, a life of Beethoven and envied his power of drawing
up into his score by constant revision and correction themes which
resisted being brought to the surface. I imagine that for her correction meant simply shaking the kaleidoscope and producing a
new, more appropriate passage.

Perhaps because Virginia lacked the novelist's sense for the dramatic properties of character and was more interested in the texture of people's minds, she was much given to drawing them
out and documenting herself upon them. She asked me a great
many questions – why I had come to live here, what I felt about
this and that, and what my ideas were about writing. I was conscious that I was being studied and even quizzed a little and also
that she and Leonard were trying to decide whether I showed
any signs of having literary talent. If so, I must publish with
them. Yet it must not for a moment be thought that she was
patronizing. On the contrary her deference to the views of the
callow and rather arrogant youth with whom she was staying
was quite surprising. She argued with me about literature, de-
fended Scott, Thackeray and Conrad against my attacks, disagreed
with my high opinion of *Ulysses* on the grounds that great works
of art ought not to be so boring,[1] and listened humbly to my

criticisms of her own novels. That was the great thing about 'Bloomsbury' – they refused to stand on the pedestal of their own age and superiority. And her visit was followed by a succession of highly characteristic letters in which she continued the theme of our discussions.

I want to emphasize Virginia's real friendliness on this occasion and the trouble she took to advise and encourage me, because her recklessness in conversation – when she was overexcited she talked too much from the surface of her mind – made some people think that she lacked ordinary sympathies. I was young for my age, and rather earnest. The isolation in which I lived had made me self-centred, and like all people who are starved for conversation I was very talkative. She on the other hand was a writer of great distinction, approaching the height of her powers. Yet she and her husband not only concealed the impatience they must often have felt, but treated me as though I was their intellectual equal. Of course, one might say, they believed in encouraging young writers and spotting the winners among them. Virginia had a strong sense of the continuity of literary tradition and felt it a duty to hand on what she had received. She was also intensely and uneasily aware of the existence of a younger generation who would one day rise and sit in judgement on her. It may be, therefore, that she thought that my strange way of life and my passion for literature showed that I might have something to give. If so, however, both she and Leonard decided a few years later that they had been mistaken.

As I sit here, trying to collect my scattered memories of this fortnight, a few scenes come before me with vividness. I recall Virginia's face in the firelight, then the gaily bantering tone in which she spoke, and Leonard's easy, companionable one. Her manner at such times was vivaciously, though rather chillily, feminine, and her voice seemed to preen itself with self-confidence in its own powers. With a little encouragement it would throw off a casacade of words like the notes of a great pianist improvising, and without the affectation – born of delight in verbal mastery – that sometimes crept into the style of her novels. Leonard, on the other hand, was very steady, very masculine – a pipe-smoking tweed-dressing man who could conduct an argument to a finish without losing the thread and who had what is called at Cambridge 'a good mind'. Morever – and this impressed me more than anything – he could read Aeschylus without a crib.

Then, scrambling on the hillside among the fig trees and the olives, I see a rather different person. An English lady, countrybred and thin, her wide-open eyes scanning the distance, who has completely forgotten herself in her delight at the beauty of the landscape and at the novelty of finding herself in such a remote and Arcadian spot. She seemed, though quiet, as excited as a schoolgirl on a holiday, while her husband's serious, sardonic features had become almost boyish. On these walks they talked of themselves and of their life together with great frankness – to have no secrets from friends was another 'Bloomsbury' characteristic – and among other things I recall Virginia telling me how incomplete she felt in comparison to her sister Vanessa, who brought up a family, managed her house, and yet found plenty of time left in which to paint. Although I doubt if she ever lost this sense of her own inadequacy, of not being quite, in every sense of the word, a person of flesh and blood, she was practical and could cook and run a house better than most women, as well as lead a social life that often probably outran her strength. . . .

It used to be said by those who were not invited to its parties that 'Bloomsbury' was a mutual admiration society who pushed one another's works. This charge, which has recently been repeated, is simply not true. Virginia Woolf greatly admired E. M. Forster's novels, which seemed to her to have the qualities of 'reality' which she perhaps felt hers lacked, and she also admired Roger Fry's writings on art as well as his marvellously eager and stimulating conversation.[2] But she had a poor opinion of Lytton Strachey's biographies, though she was greatly attached to him personally, and praised the fineness and subtlety of his mind and his discrimination as a critic. One evening, I remember, while the Woolfs were at Yegen, the subject of his *Queen Victoria* came up.[3] Both Leonard and Virginia pronounced decisively against it, declaring that it was unreadable. Although I did not care for its flat, spongy style, which gave me the sensation of walking on linoleum, this charge seemed to me absurd: readable was precisely what it was. Yet they maintained that they had been unable to finish it. Lytton, on the other hand, greatly admired most of Virginia's writings, but could not read Forster in spite of his strong personal friendship for him. I remember him saying, after looking through his little guide to Alexandria, *Pharos and Pharillon*, that it was a pity that he had taken to novel-writing when he was so much better at history.[4] And he disliked both Roger Fry and his work.

Virginia had much to say of T. S. Eliot, of whom she was seeing a good deal at this time. She praised him warmly as a man,
and spoke of his remarkable intelligence, but seemed a little half-
hearted about *The Waste Land*, which the Hogarth Press was then
publishing. Like myself, she had a poor opinion of D. H. Lawrence.
The boring prophetic mantle he wore, the streams of slovenly
and sentimental writing that poured from his pen obscured the
sometimes extraordinary freshness of insight that showed itself
in one or two of his novels and short stories. Nor had his admirers
helped his reputation, for as usually happens in such cases, they
had been more impressed by his bad books – those which contained his 'message' – than by his good ones. Yet she could change
her mind, and when, some years later, she came across *Sons and
Lovers*, she wrote an article on it which, though perhaps not very
understanding, praised it highly.[5] Has there ever been an age,
one might ask, in which writers have admired more than one or
two of their contemporaries?

*   *   *

There was a sequel [to the Woolfs' visit]. Leonard wished to return by the east-coast route and so, because he spoke little Spanish,
he pressed me to accompany them as far as Valencia. There was
always a risk to be taken in travelling with Virginia because if
she got overtired or did not sleep at nights she was apt to fall ill.
We set off therefore by bus for Almeria and next morning took
another bus which connected with the train to Murcia at Huercal
Overa. Leonard and I sat on the roof, holding on tight to keep
our seats as the clumsy conveyance lurched about, while Virginia
sat inside, choking in the clouds of dust that we churned up. It
was a wonderful drive through a desert landscape, either corrugated
and ravined like the face of the moon or else rimmed by delicate
rose and ochre hills as sharp and bare as the skeletons of ani-
mals – then suddenly interrupted by plunges into shallow, cliff-
bordered valleys where the sickly scent of orange blossom saturated
the air and tall palm trees rose out of green fields of alfalfa. Leonard
appeared to enjoy it immensely and I was only sorry that Virginia
should see so little. We slept in Murcia, where a strong stench of
drains mingled poetically with the scent of orange and lemon
blossom, and on the following day we continued to Valencia. Here
I left them and started on my way back.

NOTES

Edward Fitzgerald Brenan (1894–1987), writer. Involved romantically with Dora Carrington, Brenan mingled with the Bloomsbury Group. He spent much of his life in Spain and in addition to volumes of auto-biography published translations and works on Spain and Spanish literature.

1. The Hogarth Press had considered publishing *Ulysses* (1922) by the Irish novelist James Joyce (1882–1941) but declined it because of its length. See *Letters*, II, 242–3.
2. Edward Morgan Forster (1879–1970), novelist, short-story writer and essayist. Roger Eliot Fry (1866–1934), painter and art critic, Slade Professor of Fine Art at Cambridge. Virginia Woolf published a biography of Fry in 1940.
3. Published in 1921.
4. On Alexandria, Forster published *Pharos and Pharillon* (1923), a collection of essays and journalism, and *Alexandria: A History and a Guide* (1922).
5. 'Notes on D. H. Lawrence', *The Moment and Other Essays. Sons and Lovers* was published in 1913.

A Woman of Distinction*

SIR OSBERT SITWELL

Tonight, at Monty Shearman's[1], the Bloomsbury Junta was in full session. In later years, towards the moment of its disintegration, Bloomsbury, under the genial vice-royalty of my friend Clive Bell, took a trend, hitherto unexpected, towards pleasure and fashion-able life: but in these days it was still austere, with a degree of Quaker earnestness latent in it. (But then Roger Fry, its leading and most engaging esthetic apostle, came of Quaker stock.) The women were of a type different from that to be seen elsewhere. Something of the Victorian past clung to them still, though they were so much more advanced than their sisters, in both views and intelligence. Virginia Woolf, for instance, notably beautiful

---

* From *Laughter in the Next Room* (Boston: Little, Brown, 1948; London: Macmillan, 1949) pp. 22–4.

with a beauty of bone and form and line that belonged to the
stars rather than the sun, manifested, in her appearance, in spite
of the modernity that was also clearly hers, a Victorian distinction. She made little effort to bring out the quality of her looks,
but she could not destroy it. With her high forehead, fine, aqui-
line nose and deep-set, sculptural eye sockets, it has often occurred to me, when I have seen Roman patrician busts of the
fourth century, how greatly she resembled them. Her beauty was
certainly impersonal, but it was in no way cold, and her talk was
full of ineffable fun and lightness of play and warmth. I have
never known anyone with a more sensitive perception of the
smallest shadows cast in the air round her: nor could I ever understand why people were – but certainly they *were* – frightened
of her; because, though there was, and I am sure she would have
admitted it, a human amount of malice in her composition (and
how greatly the dull-minded would have complained if there had
not been!), there was very much more, and most unusual, gentle-
ness. To the young, to poets and painters, but not to dons, she
was invariably kind; kind, moreover, to the extent that in spite
of the burden of her own work and correspondence, she would
take trouble for them. She would, I am aware, for I have been
present, lay traps for the boastful and the blunted, and greatly
she enjoyed the snaring of them (I once had great difficulty in
rescuing alive a popular American novelist, whose name was at
that time written as a sky-sign round the roofs of Cambridge
Circus): but they deserved their fate. She possessed, too, a beautiful, clear, gentle speaking voice. Though sometimes, when many
people were present, she could be seen swaying a little, prepar-
ing herself with nervous effort, to say the words, to break through
the reserve that lay over her, yet I have heard her dare to make
a speech! It was at a dinner for the London Group of painters
about a year later than the party. Roger Fry, who was president
or chairman, had asked me to be present and to speak. When I
arrived, I found, to my great pleasure, that I was sitting next to
Virginia. But she was pitiably nervous that night because of the
prospect of having to make a speech; her distress was obvious. I
felt miserable on her behalf and, indeed, tried to comfort her: for
after having just fought an election, oratory held temporarily few
terrors for me. I concluded – and it may have been the case –
that she was unused to the strain of these occasions, and had
only consented to speak because Roger was one of her oldest

friends. If so, what happened was the more astonishing. I spoke first, and adequately, I hope, in a matter-of-fact way. The audience laughed at the jokes I made. Then I sat down, and the moment I had dreaded for Virginia arrived. She stood up. The next quarter of an hour was a superb display of art and, more remarkable, of feeling, reaching heights of fantasy and beauty in the description of the Marriage of Music to Poetry in the time of the Lutenists, and how, in the coming age, Painting must be similarly united to the other arts. It was a speech, beautifully prepared, yet seemingly spontaneous, excellently delivered, and as natural in its flow of poetic eloquence as is a peacock spreading its tail and drumming. Somehow, I had not foreseen this bravura; it was a performance that none present will ever forget, and, as she sat down, I almost regretted the sympathy I had wasted on her.

NOTES

Francis Osbert Sacheverell Sitwell (1892–1969), poet, writer of fiction and travel writer. Sitwell is perhaps best known for his five-volume autobiography (1945–9).

1. Montague Shearman (1857–1930; knighted 1914), judge. The occasion recalled occurred in November 1919.

Tavistock Square*

LOGAN PEARSALL SMITH

After the outbreak of the new war in 1939, a new epoch, I felt had dawned – or rather darkened – upon us. The best thing to do, I decided, was to begin – or to try at least to begin – a new life in these shadows. And when my friends all fled from the overcast city, I looked about to see what others I could find to replace them. But it isn't easy to make new friends when the middle years are over; such makeshifts being too often, as Chamfort[1]

* *Orion: A Miscellany* (London: Nicolson & Watson, 1945), II, 73–86.

says, like the false teeth, glass eyes and wooden legs with which those who are no longer young try in vain to repair their losses. Where in the bombed streets could I discover houses as pleasant as those whose doorbells I had been accustomed to ring? Doorbells now and then (though I hope not too often) of Mayfair houses – for on worldly scenes, the Golden Calves and the Dancing, I find I can gaze, when invited, with eyes more mild than those of Moses; or much more frequently the abodes of well-endowed, not unfashionable, yet not worldly widows or spinsters, who, being for the most part untrammelled by matrimonial ties, and free to choose their companions and say what they think, are the best hostesses, and true Queens, if they only knew it, of good company in London. I missed my agreement, and almost more my disagreement with these *doctes pucelles*, as Gil Blas[2] called such free-spoken ladies. From the country they would write me now and then; for the rest I had my memories to fall back on, and a certain number of old letters which I had saved from the salvage. – But one collection of letters I couldn't find: how on earth could I have thrown into the dust-bin my correspondence with the most beautiful, most implacable and best letter-writer of all these fastidious ladies?

Founded years ago on a family alliance, and nourished by a certain liking for each other's way of writing, a curious kind of relationship had blossomed, cactus-like, between Virginia Woolf and myself; one of those minglings of friendship and *malice* which add to the exasperation of life, but still more to its interest. Now and then we wrote to each other, and now and then I would go to see her. She would seem embarrassed, shy, almost hostile, but always polite in her stately way; nor could the visitor forget that beauty which had been for generations an inheritance of her mother's family. A gift of the Gods, some had thought it; not at all, a Family Curse, Virginia Woolf had more than once insisted, since owing to this fairness of aspect many women of her race had made grand, unsuitable, and almost always unhappy marriages; while those of them whose heads were furnished with brains rather than with coronets, had found themselves shut away into harems of gallantry, and thus deprived of opportunities for rational discourse.

On paradoxes such as this Virginia Woolf loved to expatiate; and sometimes, when she began talking, she would soar so far above the world, that to one listener at least she would seem to

be wandering, like Shelley's moon, companionless, among beings
of another birth.

It was this lunar remoteness, this disdain, like that of Artemis
with her bow of silver, which made a friend of hers, who knew
her much better than I did, write that friendship with Mrs Woolf
had always been difficult and dangerous; and the greater its intimacy, had added, the greater the danger.

Still Mrs Woolf and I were friends, or at least enemy-friends, a
good many years, and such friendships I enjoy almost as much
as warmer attachments; and even after I had become conscious
of a deepening chill in the air when we met, we still wrote to
one another now and then. I remembered those letters, written
with beautiful penmanship on dark-blue paper; and I was sorry
to hear that the salvage cart had carried off the contents of my
dust-bin. Still wasn't it just possible that this packet had escaped?
A special search was made in the cellar; and a few days later a
blue packet was placed on my table, in which I found some of
Mrs Woolf's letters, and copies of several of my answers to them.
Mrs Woolf's fame as a novel-writer and as an essayist is beyond
question, but in my opinion it is as a letter-writer that she will
be best remembered; as one of the best English letter-writers in
an age when it is supposed that good letters are no longer written. A precious volume of her letters will, I hope, be one day
published; a few of those in my possession Mr Leonard Woolf
has kindly allowed me to print.

The first of these letters was written when Virginia was living
at Richmond, at Hogarth House, in which residence she and her
husband had installed a private printing-press and had started
an amateur publishing business. This business had proved a success; Virginia had set up with her own hands a few stories of her
own and her husband's, for the marketing of which I had distributed some notices among my friends. She wrote thanking me
for this, and thanking me, too kindly perhaps, for the copy of a
book of mine (just then published) which I had sent her; she asked
me also to send her with a view to publication some Bible stories
which I had told her I had written for the edification of children;
stories of how Joshua made the sun stand still; how David peeped
at Bathsheba with her clothes off; how the whale swallowed Jonah;
how Elisha bade the bears eat up the children who mocked at
his baldness; and other Biblical incidents which might warn and
edify Sunday School children.

Thursday, Oct 23rd, 1919.

Dear Mr Pearsall Smith,

It was very good of you to send me your book.

I can't say anything intelligent about it, because I've not yet done more than look here & there; but I have hopes of saying something intelligent, so you see what pleasure you have given me already. For some reason, I have had all my time wasted these last few days, but I keep taking your book up & looking at it. It will, I know, be full of the things I most enjoy. What a lovely piece of printing it is!

We have just made out a scheme for your Bible stories, & are going to send them to the Pelican press. I liked your preface – I can't say that I believed in it.

Yours sincerely,
Virginia Woolf

These *Stories from the Old Testament* were published by the Hogarth Press in 1922. In this year Mrs Woolf's novel *Jacob's Room*, was published, and in answer to a letter from me about it she wrote:

Hogarth House,
Paradise Road,
Richmond, Surrey.
26th Oct., 1922.

Dear Mr Pearsall Smith,

It is very good of you to like *Jacob's Room*, & I am much pleased that you should. I don't think it is quite a success, but I hope (perhaps vainly) that the next one will be. The effort of breaking with complete representation sends one flying into the air. Next time I shall stick like a leech to my hero, or heroine. But please excuse this egotism.

Yours very sincerely,
Virginia Woolf

At the end of 1924, Virginia Woolf and her husband, finding
that their publishing business was still rapidly expanding, moved
from Richmond to London, taking a house in Bloomsbury large
enough to provide not only premises for their business, but a
residence as well for themselves.³ This house was in Tavistock
Square, near which were the homes of those friends of theirs who
were commonly known as the 'Bloomsbury' writers; and it so
happened that when Mr and Mrs Woolf 'set up shop', as it were,
in London, this group of authors had put themselves before a
new public, being invited to do so by a lady who had come from
America to edit the London edition of an American fashion paper.
This lady, having intellectual interests, had offered generous terms
to the intellectuals of Bloomsbury to contribute to the columns of
this publication. All of them I think (with the exception of Lytton
Strachey) responded with alacrity to her offers. One afternoon,
when calling in Tavistock Square, I happened to express the opinion
that journalism of this kind might be detrimental to authors of
promise, who, if they habitually wrote for people of fashion, might
very likely end by writing carelessly. That the audience one wrote
for could not but affect one's way of writing was Mrs Woolf's
opinion, I took for granted; but now, to my astonishment, my
chance remark roused her to one of those outbursts of defiance
which Duncan Grant, writing of her after her death, said she sometimes inflicted on her friends.⁴ Certainly I was not spared upon
this occasion. It was I and my associates, it was people like Gosse
and Robert Bridges,⁵ and all the respectabilities and solemnities
and humbugs who wrote for papers like the *Times Literary Supplement*, who were the enemies of unfettered thought in England;
we deliberately did our best to stifle all freedom, all rebellion, all
ribaldry, in the English press. Were it not for the fashion papers,
the writers I referred to, Mrs Woolf declared, would be gagged
and suffocated; only in the columns that were put so freely at
their disposal could they feel themselves free to express what
they really thought.

The next day I received this postcard:

> 52 Tavistock Square,
> [Jan. 26, 1925]

I was too shy yesterday to put you a question which interests
me deeply.

Did you read my article in a fashion paper – 'Indiscretions';[6] & if so did you think, as an impartial critic, that it was inferior to or in any way differed from articles that I write for the *Nation*? Much depends upon your answer.

Virginia Woolf

I wrote in reply that I hadn't seen the article she mentioned, adding that I wouldn't of course have spoken as I had done of that journal if I had the dimmest notion that she was among the contributors to its fashionable columns. With this note I sent her some American books I had promised to lend her. She wrote:

52 Tavistock Square,
London, W.C.I.
Jan. 30, 1925.

Dear Logan,

It is very good of you to send me the books, & to bother to make enquiries. It will be a great help to me, as I am completely at sea about modern American literature.

I am sorry your visit was so disagreeable to you – one ought to leave a tea party happier not more miserable. But you have the laugh of me. I had planned such a trap for you – I did send one article to the paper you mentioned, but it was intended for the *Nation*, & just about to be printed, when the editor became clamorous, & rather than write specially for her, I snatched it from Leonard, to his fury. And I hoped you would detect signs of the fashion papers in every word.

I am in bed with the influenza (which I hope I did not give you – perhaps that accounts for my disagreeableness the other day) & have been ruminating the whole question of the *Lit. Sup.* & Robert Bridges & respectability & Mayfair. On top of my ruminations comes a letter from a young man, who writes for the *Lit. Sup.*, complaining that they have cut a very mildly irreverent story from his last review. That sort of thing does seem to me bad for young writers – perhaps worse than the vulgarity, which is open & shameless, of the fashion papers. Anyhow, the young would say, they let you write what you like, & it's your own fault if you conform to the stays & the petticoats. Then, Duncan says he is perfectly ready to paint covers for them or ballrooms for Lady E. – who doesn't know one picture from another, & has a drawing-room filled with the riff-raff of London (I hope this does not hurt your feelings). Duncan's argument is that if Bloomsbury has real pearls, they can be scattered anywhere without harm. Perhaps we aren't quite sure of our pearls – I don't know. It is all very complicated. One thing emerges however – except for a few stars, who are paid what they ask, their prices are exactly the same as the *Nation*'s.

Forgive this tedious & influenza letter, & do not allow my perversities to prevent you from coming again.

Yours very sincerely,
Virginia Woolf

This descent from the high towers of Bloomsbury of its inhabitants had inspired me, in the meantime, to celebrate their introduction into fashionable journalism in an article entitled 'Preaching to Butterflies',[7] which was published by Leonard Woolf in the *Nation* (of which he was then the literary editor), and in this article I wrote as follows:

Whether on account of the mutable nature of Fashion's ideal, or because its object is not beauty but exclusiveness, and is discarded as soon as others attain it; or because it aims at adorning the body, rather than the soul (which some hold the better part) – for these reasons, or perhaps because they cut so poor a figure in it, our moral essayists have always been vociferous in their reprobation of Vanity Fair; they have no words strong enough to condemn it; Hazlitt devoted one of his most indignant essays to the subject. 'Fashion', he declaims, 'is the abortive issue of vain ostentation and exclusive egotism: it is haughty, trifling, affected, servile, despotic, mean'.[8] But what a way is this of talking to these Fairies? St Francis preached to the birds, but he did not, I believe, trouble the butterflies with his sermons. If there be need for their enlightenment, much more do I praise the amenity of the group of our modern writers, who, in their commiseration of the benighted state of fashion's victims (and it is impossible of course, to imagine any other motive), have condescended to shed the lustre of their minds upon its journals, nor deemed it beneath the dignity of letters to insert, between

articles on Cosmetics, and advertisements of Exclusive Under-
wear, little snippets and butterfly-dishes of Art and Culture.
And their fluttering beneficiaries, thus enabled to echo in their
tiny voices the latest cries of the most superior circles, have
erected in gratitude an exquisite Temple of Fame for their bene-
factors in their fairy kingdom. To this the chosen ones send in
their photographs, and these are printed in the Fashion Papers,
and thus given the widest publicity. Nothing could be more
genial, more in accordance with the high traditions of our literature; and those of us who are excluded must do nothing to
disparage or trouble in any way this felicitous *entente*.

This article, though kindly meant, was, I believe, resented by
the writer referred to. An attempt was made to procure my photograph to reproduce in the *Hall of Fame*, which was to be renamed
Hall of Shame for this occasion. This attempt failed; but it happened by chance to coincide with a falling off in circulation of
one fashion paper, whose readers took no interest, it appeared,
in the articles written by the Bloomsbury Intellectuals. Their clever
and learned contributions were no longer printed, and the policy
of the paper was changed. Whether Mrs Woolf had been annoyed
by what I had written I never knew – we never discussed the
matter. Not long after, however, she renewed her request that I
should send something to the Hogarth Press for them to publish.
   Thereupon I wrote a brief essay, entitled 'The Prospects of Literature', in which I described what I considered the unhappy condi-
tion of literature at that time in England, and sketched the kind
of life which I thought a man of letters might still lead, and the
kind of books which he might successfully write, even in these,
to my mind, untoward circumstances. This pamphlet was published by the Hogarth Press in 1927, and aroused not the slightest
interest. Undiscouraged by this failure, Mrs Woolf asked me, when
I called on her one afternoon, to write for them at greater length
a tract on this subject. I happened to speak rather vaguely of the
publication some day of various essays of mine to be collected in
one volume; and Mrs Woolf suggested that this book should be
published by the Hogarth Press.
   About this time I began to feel conscious, however, of the chill
I have mentioned in the air when I went to Tavistock Square.
Perhaps Virginia had never quite forgiven my remarks about the
fashion papers, or (what is more likely) she had lost interest in

the company and conversation of one who was so much older than herself. When, having written the essay on Imaginative Prose she had suggested, I sent her a note saying that I should like to come to Tavistock Square to discuss it, she either did not reply to this note, or replied after so long a delay, or in such terms that I thought it better to let the matter drop; and after some years I sent the scattered essays I had now collected to other publishers, and not to the Hogarth Press. I needed, however, the Press's permission to reprint an essay which Mrs Woolf had published, and in writing to her I took the opportunity of expressing my regret that we no longer met, after so many years of acquaintance. My letter and her answer appear as follows in the packet:

[1932]

Dear Virginia,

I am thinking of following your example (I am reading your essays in *The Common Reader* with the enchantment with which I read all your writings) in collecting together my various essays in a volume which Constable have agreed to publish.[9] As one of these, 'The Prospects of Literature', was printed by you, I wonder if I could come to some arrangement with the Hogarth Press about it? I would gladly purchase the unsold copies if I might recover the copyright in this manner, and thus your books would be relieved of a bothersome little account.

My *Stories from the Old Testament* which you also published, is now, I believe, out of print. Does this give me the right to print them again? I should like to do so, as I find they have helped many to find salvation, and I have thus been carrying on trade of saving souls, and hope to wear these diamonds in my heavenly crown. Of rubies I shall have an abundance, since a tract published by my father long ago, called *How Little Logan was Brought to Jesus*, recounts how my sister Mary and a little friend of hers took me at the age of four into our bathroom and accomplished, by means of earnest prayer, my conversion. This tract had an enormous circulation at the time, and produced an especially powerful effect on the Red Indians of the West, who were quite unable to withstand it.

[1932]

Dear Logan,

I gave your letter to Leonard, and I think he has answered you. I'm glad you are collecting your essays, though sorry that they are going to Constable. If by any chance you want to reprint *How Little Logan Found Jesus*, I shall be proud to publish it – indeed I will print it with my own hands, if only to carry on the work of conversion and find a shorter way to heaven myself.

[1932]

Dear Virginia,

Thank you for your letter – Leonard has replied most kindly to my requests.

I should indeed be proud if you would reprint the tract of my conversion. I will have a look and see if I can find a copy. If it should help you also to salvation, what a jewel I should have to blaze in my crown in heaven!

By the way, are we enemies? My memory isn't very good in these matters, but I seem to recollect that when I wrote some years ago, asking if I might come to see you, I received a rather frosty answer – or was it no answer at all? Anyhow, I have often regretted that I never see you.

Oct. 31st [1932]

Dear Logan,

I am sorry not to have written before, but I have been very busy – our clerks always fall ill at the critical moment – and indeed all I have to say is that for my part I was not conscious that we were 'enemies' as you suggest. My memory is probably as bad as yours, and I have no recollection of not answering your suggestion that you should come and see me. I am very sorry if I was so forgetful. I think it possible, though, as we live in a world of gossip, that some rumour had reached me that you were not favourably disposed to Bloomsbury – why should you be? – and I felt that there would be a certain discomfort in meeting, at least on my side. This is the only explanation that occurs to me of our not meeting oftener, and of course I regret it as much as you do.

Nov. 2 [1932]

Dear Virginia

Thanks for your letter. Do not be alarmed by the thought that I am proffering an olive branch, I only want to say that I don't think that I have ever been really hostile to Bloomsbury. I have always thought, and sometimes said (to the intense annoyance of my hearers) that I regarded Bloomsbury as the only group of free spirits in the English-speaking race. I may have mocked at Bloomsbury, since mockery is my favourite pastime, and also perhaps (to take a darker peep into that dark cabinet, the human heart) because I was not admitted to its conclaves. That I have told funny stories about it is possible, nor is it utterly inconceivable that I may have invented one or two. I see in the tract of my conversion (I have found a copy) that my little sister's first prayer, when we knelt together, was as follows: 'O Lord, please make little Logan a good boy, and don't let him tell any more lies'.

Her little friend then prayed, 'Lord, please give Logan a new heart', and little Logan earnestly echoed her prayer in these words, 'Lord Jesus, please give me a new heart'.

It would appear however that the prayers of these little maidens, and of my little (and better) self have not been really answered, so I must get on as best I can with my old heart – unless you can recommend a heart specialist who can treat my case.

So there it is, and there it must remain. I know from my own feelings how justly critics resent criticism, and mockers being mocked.

I have been reading with great interest what you say about Fulke Greville in your book.[10] I read his aphorisms some years ago; they are (like almost all collections of this kind, except those of la Rochefoucauld) of a devastating dullness, but having a perverted taste for this kind of literature, I copied out a few which I thought may interest you.

Those who listen to themselves, are not listened to by others.

A proud man never shews his pride so much as when he is civil.

To divest one's self of some prejudices would be like taking off the skin to feel the better.

It was supposed at the time, I believe, that Mrs Greville wrote these aphorisms: but this I can hardly believe, since no woman except George Eliot has been mistress of this delicate art.
With this little pin-prick to end my letter, I remain *etc.*

Nov. 6 [1932]

Dear Logan,

Do not be alarmed, to quote your own words, by the thought that I am proffering an olive branch. And excuse the typewriter, but my hand is getting too illegible for prolonged use. Confined to my sofa at the moment – how apposite your reference to a heart specialist was! – I have been pondering your letter, certain aspects of which interested me greatly; so that I can't resist writing, though I fear longwindedly, but then I'm rather knocked up.

I agree with you that one can admire a set or group and at the same time indulge a malicious desire to laugh at it. Am I not just as guilty as you are? Only of course I laugh at Chelsea whereas you laugh at Bloomsbury. And I feel great admiration and respect for Chelsea as you do for Bloomsbury – indeed I can't see any reason for you to prefer Bloomsbury, as you intimate you do; but then, alas, so much of what you say is ironical. And I, too, have always thought and I have often said (to quote you again) to the great annoyance of people like Lady D. and Mrs K. who (you know what great ladies are) sometimes sneer at Chelsea – that in my opinion it is full of delightful people and brilliant gatherings. How could it not be? I need only mention, besides yourself, Desmond, Maurice Baring,[11] Ethel Sands, Bob and Hilda Trevelyan, Mr Connolly, Mrs Hammersley: and then there's Lady Colefax round the corner. How can you, even in politeness, put us in Bloomsbury above you? I'm sure you don't. It's only your fun. But much though I admire Chelsea, I freely admit that I have mocked at you all, because mockery is 'my favourite pastime', just as it is yours. And I may have made up a story or two about you into the bargain.

Up to this point there is not much difference between us.

Now comes the interesting distinction. I have known Chelsea for many years. For many years they have asked me to tea and dinner and I have asked them to tea and dinner. And then I discovered that they were laughing at me and my friends behind my back; and they discovered that I was laughing at them and their friends behind their backs. So I gave up asking them; and I gave up accepting their invitations. This is not due to having a good heart – it is simply that such intercourse seemed to me dull, barren, fruitless, uninteresting.

Now what I find so interesting is that you, who are, as far as I can make out, in the same case as I am, will yet take the trouble to write to me and say 'perhaps we are enemies?' You will write like this implying – but again, in dealing with so ironical a mind how careful one must be not to exaggerate – still such words do seem to me to imply that you would actually like to come and see me. Yes, I turn to your first letter, and there you say in so many words 'I often regret that I never see you'. Now is this true, or is it ironical? And how can you like seeing me, if you laugh at me and my friends behind my back?

These are some of the questions that I ponder as I lie here. And, thus pondering, it seems to me possible that you are right – at least to this extent. That is, why should not Chelsea and Bloomsbury meet and laugh at each other to their faces and quite genuinely enjoy themselves? It seems to me worth trying. Then again, you say 'critics resent criticism and mockers being mocked'. But do they, if it's done face to face? Surely both sides might benefit greatly if it were done in that way.

I am ashamed to see that I have written all this without making, or quoting, a single aphorism. And how delightful your little galaxy of them from – is it Fulke Greville? – is at the end of your letter! I have racked my brains to think of one to end with; but am relieved to have it on your authority that 'no woman (except George Eliot) was mistress of this delicate art'. So be it. I will leave aphorisms to your sex. With regard to the pin-prick – 'with this little pin-prick to end my letter' – to quote you again, my trouble is that either through age or habit I have become almost impervious to pin-pricks. If you want to rub them in you will have to prick a good deal harder. And I promise, if you will come and see me, that I'll rummage in my dressing table for a few pins of my own. I'm sure you don't intend to claim pin-pricking as an exclusively masculine art.

There, to quote you once more, we must leave it. Come and laugh at me and my work and my friends to my face, and I'll do the same by you. No doubt we shall both profit. I am not allowed at present to do much entertaining, but in two or three weeks I shall be delighted to see you on the terms stated, I fear rather diffusely, above.

Yours very sincerely,
Virginia Woolf

On reading this over, I see that the molehill has become a mountain – but then the molehill was raised by you.

Nov. 12, 1932.

My Dear Virginia,

Your letter gave me great pleasure; and I like to cling to the belief that it was an olive branch, as indeed my own letters were, though I mingled a little bitter myrrh with them, so that you could take them in another sense, if you preferred. But the things I said about Bloomsbury and about my regret at never seeing you were not in the least ironical, and came from the truest corner of that unsanctified heart, which, in spite of all the praying, I have never been able somehow to change for a better one. So some day I do hope you will let me come and see you. Why, as you say, shouldn't we mock at each other before each other's faces? I love mockery so much, that I am delighted even when I am myself its subject. Things said of me behind my back I don't enjoy, and don't listen to them.

I am sorry that you aren't well; I spend a good deal of my time in a dull kind of invalidism, so that I can feel sympathy with you. But these spells end; one does emerge sooner or later from the dark tunnel; and I hope that this will soon happen to you. In the meantime I have been copying out for you the tract of my conversion, or I should have written sooner. But just when I had finished making my copy, the Poltergeist or little devil which hides my pens, pencils, scissors and spectacles every day, stole the neat little booklet, hid it in the chaos of non-existence which lies so close round each of us, and I can't find it anywhere, though I have searched every conceivable place a

hundred times. I thought it might be a comfort and means of
help to you in your illness, and shall now have the original
type-written at once, and send you a copy. I think it must be
reprinted, though I can hardly flatter myself that you will under-
take the task. But since it saved so many Red Indians in its
time, might it not possibly help to salvation some of the Apaches
and *jeunes féroces* of a region of London which I shall not name?
I have a charming photograph of the holy little Logan which
would make a delightful illustration for it.

Speaking of Bloomsbury (but have I been speaking of it?) I
think the Irish saying might be quoted 'Distant cows have long
horns', for I have never seen the long horns which you appear
to have discerned across the intervening regions of Mayfair,
while you say that the horns which we see so formidably looming
in Bloomsbury are equally non-existent. Perhaps when we meet
we shall turn out to be harmless, hornless creatures, with nothing
but love for each other. But one admission I will make; Chelsea is a little infected by its proximity to Mayfair; over it hangs
the stern verdict which I expressed in my little book of Aphorisms as follows:

'You cannot be both fashionable and first-rate'. Not that we
are really fashionable in Chelsea, but we want to be, and you
don't.

I met the other day a beautiful young Queen of Mayfair, who
was, she told me, passionately devoted to modern literature,
and who had always believed that Chelsea and Bloomsbury
were one and the same kingdom, with Rebecca West for its
Queen.[12] Perhaps this is the ultimate truth; it will at any rate
serve as a pin-prick (though it pricks us all) with which to end
this letter.

Nov. 27, 1932.

Dear Logan,

I am a wretch not to have thanked you before for your letter
and the tract. I have read it with great amusement, and only
wish it were longer. Leonard has now read it too – we have
over 600 MSS. to read yearly now, which accounts for our extreme slowness; and it strikes him that you perhaps might add
an introduction and let us print it. But no doubt you won't

want to do this. But perhaps if you will come and see us one day – on the terms agreed on – we might discuss it. It is certainly edifying in the extreme; and the portrait is delightful.

Yes I agree about Chelsea. I don't like the mix up of letters and coronets. But I'm afraid there are a good many coronets in Bloomsbury now – the peerage seems to have taken us up – but as long as we don't become peers ourselves, I find the peerage intoxicatingly beautiful – the old English peerage I mean – not the rich peerage, nor – I was going to say the American peerage – would that have been a pin prick? or an aphorism?

Yours very sincerely,
Virginia Woolf

Dec. 1, 1932.

Dear Virginia,

It would indeed be delightful if you would print the tract, as I think it might do good. I should certainly write a brief introduction to it.

Anyhow, I should love to come and see you. I will bring some polished shafts from Chelsea, and hope you will have some ready from the armoury of Gordon (or Gorgon) Square. But I shall be much too timid to start the conflict, so you must strike first, if you want a fight. But why should we fight after all? Why shouldn't we all love each other?

600 MSS. to read a year! The thought staggers me out of my Christian walking. But I think I have an explanation. I met the other day a female wielder of the pen, who told me that she had signed contracts to write in the next year:

(1) An enormous novel, dealing with religion *au fond*.
(2) Series of broadcast talks on food, with pamphlet.
(3) A life of Lady Jane Gray (£200 paid in advance).
(4) A translation of several vols. of *Le Tableau de Paris*.
(5) A large compendium for house wives on food, clothing, dressmaking, upholstering, the care of drains, with hints on children, and how to keep husbands at home.
(6) A life of Captain Cook.
(7) A detective story in collaboration with Clemence Dane,[13] the intervals to be filled with lectures and articles for the *Spectator*.

Now my theory is (I may be wrong) that the books you read are all written by this lady, who out-writes you and out-runs you in the glorious race of glory – that she writes on faster than you can read. Am I right?

I will not end this letter with a pin-prick, which is after all a horrid way of writing, but with a perfectly irrelevant thought which occurred to me this morning. Here it is: one of the sayings of Little Logan, 'If you are losing your leisure, look out, you may be losing your soul'.

Dec. 4, 1932.

Dear Logan,

I am afraid that, as this week is very full, it will have to be the week after. Perhaps tea, 4.30, on Thursday 15th will suit you.

I am quite ready to 'love' as you suggest; the idea of fighting originated with you I fancy. At least I seem to remember a remark of yours to the effect that we must have quarrelled because I had not asked you to tea. Let it be 'love' by all means.

And of course, though I am unable to invent aphorisms, I try to understand those of others, and I take the meaning of your latest and loveliest – 'If you are losing your leisure, look out! – it may be you are losing your soul', to be that these letters waste a good deal of time; and that it is extremely good of you to lose still more leisure, and imperil your soul by coming all this way to tea. I do so profoundly agree.

Therefore do not trouble to answer. We shall look forward to seeing you on Thursday the 15th unless I hear to the contrary.

I went on the 15th, but my welcome, though polite, did not make me feel inclined to make again the journey between Chelsea and Tavistock Square. 'A few yards in London,' Sydney Smith once wrote, 'dissolve or make a friendship'.[14] The distance between my home and that of Mrs Woolf was more than a matter of topography – it was one mainly perhaps of age; anyhow it seemed to me a vain endeavour (as she herself hinted) to make any further attempt to cross it. Though we shared many likes and even more dislikes, we didn't really hunt in the same pack, and had no overwhelming enthusiasm for each other's friends. We met at dinner occasionally, and enjoyed – at least I enjoyed – our not unfriendly conversations. Now and then we wrote to each other, on matters of impersonal interest. I remember, for instance, proposing to the BBC Committee on Spoken English that she should be asked to join that Committee, and writing to ask her if she would be willing to accept such an invitation. She replied agreeing at first to do so, but on further consideration asked me to withdraw her name; she had never, she wrote, been on a committee, and did not regard herself as an authority on linguistic or any other questions. I wrote to say of course that I would comply with her request, but I do not find in my blue packet our correspondence on this and one or two other such subjects. What I did find, oddly enough, was this paraphrase I had written of a Chinese poem 'The Jade Staircase', by Li Po. I feel that my correspondent was not unlike this Empress.

> The stairs of jade with dew are wet,
> On this long autumn night, and yet
> With many a pause and footstep slow,
> Up in the dark the Queen must go.
> Her dress of glimmering silk, her veil,
> Drenched with the drops of silver, trail.
> Through the pavilion will she pass,
> And open the window-blind and glass;
> In will a pearly radiance pour
> And shine in pools upon the floor.
> There gazing on the moon, whose beams
> Are pale and cold as her own dreams,
> A long time leaning on her hands,
> A long, long time, the Empress stands.

NOTES

Lloyd Logan Pearsall Smith (1865–1946), American-born writer educated t Harvard University and at Balliol College, Oxford. Smith's literary career ranged widely, and in addition to writing short fiction, verse and biographies, he was a noted editor of anthologies.

1. Nicolas-Sébastien Chamfort (c. 1740–94), writer of maxims, dramatist and poet.

2. The title-character of Alain-René Lesage's picaresque romance *Gil Blas de Santillane* (published 1715–35).

3. The move occurred in March, in fact.

4. See p. 138.

5. Robert Bridges (1844–1930), poet and man of letters.

6. Published in *Vogue* in November 1924.

7. In fact, published in the *New Statesman*, 14 March 1925, pp. 655–7.

8. William Hazlitt, 'On Fashion' (1818).

9. *Reperusals and Re-Collections* (London: Constable, 1936). The collection does not reprint 'The Prospects of Literature'.

10. *The Common Reader* (2nd series).

11. Maurice Baring (1874–1945), novelist, particularly of high society.

12. Rebecca West (1892–1983; DBE 1959), pen name of Cicily Isabel, critic, reporter and author.

13. Pseudonym of Winifred Ashton (1888–1965), playwright and novelist.

14. Sydney Smith (1771–1845), lecturer and preacher, a prolific writer and one of the founders of the *Edinburgh Review*.

'Few women since the beginning of the world have equalled her'*

DORA CARRINGTON

[13 July 1921]: To Lytton Strachey We reached the Woolfs rather late for tea but of course they are so charming they never really mind and the tea was delicious. Really Virginia does make heavenly jams. Then, after tea, Leonard went for a walk over the downs with Ralph, and Virginia and I trailed behind gossiping and croaking. Mary, you and your writing (of which I knew nothing), Vanessa and Mary, Ralph and THE SITUATION,[1] the merits of Rodmell against Asheham,[2] composed our conversation. I came back filled with enthusiasm for Virginia. It's impossible not to fall in love with her I find. She was so friendly to me I couldn't help col-

---

* From *Carrington: Letters and Extracts from her Diaries*, ed. David Garnett (London: Jonathan Cape, 1970) pp. 186, 242, 245, 246, 261, 477.

lapsing completely. Dinner. Then a sogjourn – which I know is spelt wrong but I can't make it look better – to the summer house. Leonard very grave after a terrible silence. 'Well I think we had better perhaps discuss the Situation'. Then he started. Really he is superb: so logical, fair, and intelligent. Then Virginia gave her point of view. Then Ralph rather tentatively returned the fire. And I summed up the proceedings at the tail end of everything.

27 April 1923: To Gerald Brenan   I long to have news of you, and hear all about the Woolves.[3] You can't be too enthusiastic, to please me, over Virginia! I always feel she is one of the few people it has actually been tremendously good fortune to have known in this life. I am sure few women since the beginning of the world have equalled her for wit and charm, and a special rare kind of beauty.

28 May 1923: To Gerald Brenan   I was going to write to you this long letter after I had seen Virginia but then something she told me when I went to tea with her last Wednesday made everything vanish out of my head.

I wanted to go to tea with her alone, but that wasn't possible, as R[alph] was in London with me. Still it didn't make any difference really. Virginia said just as I was putting a piece of stale iced cake into my mouth, 'You know Gerald is going to get married; he has just written and told Leonard that he is engaged to that American girl'.[4] I think it was the word 'engaged' that made me feel it wasn't true and then made me rather angry. I felt Virginia couldn't know you very well to use such a word in reference to you, or perhaps everything had changed. I quickly argued that my feelings were absurd, all words are absurd and 'engaged' is just as good a word as 'bedding'. Then she said: 'I thought he probably would get married very soon, but of course it may be one of his jokes'. . . .

I told Virginia I wasn't surprised and that I guessed you would soon marry E. It was only half true. I wanted to gain a little time to hide my feelings from her. Then it is partly true for ever since you first told me about E. I had faced this as a probability.

Perhaps if you have her with you, you will be able to regard me more easily as a 'neuter' friend. It's pretty depressing what a mess I made of your feelings and of mine last year. I always thank you for not reviling me.

Virginia was so charming. But it was a slight nightmare. I longed to talk to her about you, ask her hundreds of questions.

But I felt as if there was a glass window between us and that she couldn't hear what I was saying.

15 September 1923: To Gerald Brenan Virginia and Leonard are really superb people. We visited them on our way back. I always choose the Newhaven crossing, it's such a good place to see England at its best. We drove straight to the Woolves in the car. They are only a few miles from Newhaven; Sussex *is* a wonderful county!. . . .

I like the Woolves far more than they like me. Ugh. I have a queer love for Virginia which fills me with emotion when I see her. They talk better than any people I know. How quickly the conversation becomes intelligent and amusing when Virginia talks!

[1931]: To Julia Strachey Virginia, and Leonard have just been down here for the day. They are a fascinating couple. I found Virginia's conversation irresistible. She is *very* enthusiastic about your story, and so was Leonard.[5] They gave you a tremendous high praise, your old Tante was delighted. She has been struggling with a cover, but how not to look like Mr Whistler (Rex).[6] That is the problem. How to cram in the socks, penknives, ferns, inkpots, wedding cakes and jellies. All very difficult. I suggested to Virginia that she should get *you* to illlustrate your own masterpiece (C. 'her drawings, only of course she never lets anyone see them and always crosses them out, are equal to her writing'), I regret to say Virginia refused to be lured away from her horrid intentions.

NOTES

Dora Carrington (1893–1932), painter. With her husband Reginald Ralph Partridge (1894–1960), she was the third person in a triangular relationship with Lytton Strachey, sharing a home with him at Tidmarsh and then at Ham Spray, Ham, Wiltshire. Although not members of the Bloomsbury Group, Carrington and Partridge moved in its wider circle.

1. Mary Hutchinson, née Barnes (1889–1977), related to the Stracheys, was Clive Bell's companion. Ralph Partridge was considering leaving the Hogarth Press.
2. The Woolfs had their country homes in Sussex first in Asheham and then at Monk's House, Rodmell.
3. The Woolfs were then visiting Brenan in Spain. See pp. 45–9.

4. 'This story of my engagement to an American girl must have been one of Virginia's inventions' (Gerald Brenan's note).
5. *Cheerful Weather for the Wedding* (Hogarth Press, 1932).
6. Reginald John ('Rex') Whistler (1905–44), illustrator and stage designer.

'The most remarkable human being'*

NIGEL NICOLSON

Let me say straight away that Virginia is without question the most remarkable human being that I've ever known, and I think there would be very few people who knew her at all well who wouldn't say the same. She used to come and spend a couple of nights here.[1] Often when I came back from school, I would find her here. I loved her coming, absolutely loved her.

Virginia was rather delicate. I always think of her as an indoor person. I think of her extending those long, beautiful hands to a fire in the autumn. She was extremely beautiful. Even as a child I realized that. It was a beauty which increased with age. *Never* pretty, but *lovely*.

She was very good with children. She used to write to us. Oh, my God, I wish I'd kept those letters! I remember a long letter she enclosed with her copy of *Flush*. I've got the book but I haven't got the letter. My mother would say, 'Virginia's coming tonight'. We would say, 'Oh, good!' It was always like that. She was fun. She would play with words and events, and nothing was boring to her.

And she had no conceit at all, absolutely none. She was the opposite: she distrusted her art, felt that she had failed, and minded ridiculously the criticisms of people of no importance whatever.

My mother and Virginia used to give each other presents ... six duck's eggs. Or Virginia would find a chamber pot in an antique shop and send it along. We always knew who it had come from. There was no note to say.

* From Joanne Trautmann, 'A Talk with Nigel Nicolson', *Virginia Woolf Quarterly*, vol. 1, no. 1 (Fall 1972) pp. 38–44.

We used to spend the whole day at Rodmell, and sometimes we were chased out when they wanted to talk. We used to play as children on the Downs and come back, and then there'd be this hugger-mugger sitting-room and Virginia's horrible little writing-room upstairs.

There was in Virginia a little bit of a snob, but in a Proustian sense. She liked the great swing of English history and everything, including literature and architecture, that was associated with it. She liked the feeling of this vast continuity of portraits hanging on the walls, forming a sort of second set of occupants of the house watching their descendants. Virginia was a great romantic in that way, and to meet a young woman, my mother, who was the product of one of the greatest houses and greatest families in the country, and yet was shy, intellectual, not flashy, not social ... it was for Virginia already in itself a romance. . . .

I can remember very well going to Virginia's parties at Tavistock Square as a boy. It was rather frightening. You did feel – grown-ups would have felt it even more – that you were on trial there. They would toss questions at you, and if you missed it, it was like being sacked from the team. You were no longer regarded as one of the first eleven. So my mother, who wasn't very quick intellectually – she was deep, but not quick – was, I think, a little alarmed by these parties. The tone of them was faintly malicious. There was a lot of gossip. I mean, the idea is that they were talking about the nature of the beautiful, of the good, about architecture, painting, literature the whole time. Not at all. They were talking a lot of gossip about their friends and sparing nobody.

There were always a lot of hangers-on. The central core of Bloomsbury, of course, was really pre-war. And in the twenties Bloomsbury had a sort of second wind when some of these younger people came in, but no society at all. They were all people of a middle class, even working class, background.

The world was their subject: politics, all forms of art, including the newest one, the cinema. They were passionately thrilled by the cinema. They used to go on these movie expeditions. These took place only in the evening, and all day they worked. And then occasionally they would have in some famous outsider like Wells or Bernard Shaw or someone like that. Then when he had gone, he was pulled to pieces. But it was very gay, very happy. The idea that Bloomsbury was a sort of solemn, over-intellectual society is quite, quite wrong. It was the gayest group of people that I've ever known.

What remains in my mind so clearly is the character, the texture, of the relationship between Virginia and Leonard. Leonard was tremendously solicitous to her, knowing that she was always on the point of going mad again. (I didn't know that then.) They had an almost biblical relationship. It was like Mary and Joseph. They were totally different people – Leonard the politician, Virginia the imaginative genius. In a sort of way their marriage was very like my own parents', very, very like, and for the same sorts of reasons.

Anyhow, so my mother and father entered the Bloomsbury world, and for both of them it was a tremendous excitement. In that world both my mother and my father found the two greatest friends of their lives. In my mother's case, Virginia, and in my father's case, Raymond Mortimer.[2] They continued to see their smarter friends, who were rather sneered at by Virginia in a sort of teasing way. My father became a friend of Leonard's. My mother was Virginia's friend. My father had his reservations about Virginia, and Leonard had his reservations about my mother.

The reservations weren't very strong. There was never any question of their not getting on together, all four of them. They would very frequently go to the movies together, all four. But when Virginia came here or to Longbarn,[3] it was always alone. I suppose Leonard must have come here for lunch or something. But I remember Virginia spending days here, sleeping here. My father felt, I think, that Virginia was a little too malicious; he didn't like gossip. He felt that was one side of her. But, my goodness, he recognized her genius! I don't think my father was in the least jealous of Virginia. Whatever jealousy there was in this quadrilateral relationship was Leonard being jealous of my mother. But my father had no jealousy in his nature. He wasn't jealous of my mother's writing or her success or her friends. My mother would say, 'Virginia and I are going off to France' or 'I'm going to Rodmell for a week'. 'Have a lovely time', he'd say. And then they would write to each other every day, as always.

Leonard had considerable contempt for my mother's writing, particularly her novels. In his autobiography he's very hard about *The Edwardians*.[4] He's right: my mother hadn't got genius. But she had talent. . . .

My mother had great physical energy. She was very strong and practical. In fact Virginia used to reproach my mother with being hard and worldly, half as a joke. With having these two sides to her character – which was quite true – this passionate side and this practical side. I mean, she was a poet and novelist and she was also a garden creator, ran the farm, sat on the magistrate's bench. Virginia used to tease her about this side of her, and at the same time realized that my mother had this poetic side, this deep attachment to the country and a deep attachment to English literature, out of which her writing emerged.

I don't know the circumstances [of their first meeting]. The first letter from Virginia is dated December 28, 1922. There's mention in that letter of Virginia's asking to obtain a copy of my mother's book, *Knole and the Sackvilles*.[5] I can only assume that they met at a party, that they got into conversation, and that they both knew about the other. Anyhow, they must have met with some common friends. And they talked about each other's books, you can imagine with what shyness on my mother's side – on both sides. And Virginia must have said, 'I've never read your book, *Knole and the Sackvilles*'. And my mother must have replied, 'I'll send you a copy'. The first letter at the Berg is about this book.[6] From then on it progressed, and within a couple of months – because it took quite a long time in those days – they were on Christian name terms. And then their relationship became more and more intimate.

At some point Virginia and my mother fell in love. From my reading of the letters I would guess that the relationship existed on a physical level for about four years. My mother's letters to Virginia are letters of devotion such as would be exchanged between men and women. But since the physical aspects were very little emphasized, the friendship continued to be a close and intimate one on many levels until Virginia's death.

[In *Orlando*] I'm reading a fantasy based upon my mother's ... upon Virginia's view of my mother, written at a time when they were at the height of their love affair. And Virginia, by this extraordinary magic ... I mean, today it would seem perhaps a little forced or even unoriginal, but in 1928 it was an extraordinary *tour de force* of literature. To conceive this idea of a portrait of an actual woman living today, changing sex, and being immortal! (What a marvellous film it would make!) So the concept of the book is brilliant. And at the same time the whole book is a tease.

My mother did a broadcast on *Orlando*.[7] She quoted a lot from

Virginia's letters to her while *Orlando* was being written. My mother never saw a word of *Orlando* until she received a printed copy on the eve, or on the day or two, before publication. Then she sat up the whole night reading this portrait of herself. My father was in Berlin in the embassy. Virginia sent him a copy of it the same day. And he sat up too. In the Berg Collection there's a lovely letter from my mother to Virginia, written the next morning, expressing a really staggered admiration of Virginia's art. 'How could you have done this?' Not reproachful, but 'Why can't I do this sort of thing?' It's really a marvellous letter and, in the circumstances, such a strange letter. She had been reading her own biography and yet thinking not so much about what sort of picture Virginia forms of her, but what a marvellous book it is.

So there's a sort of amused background to *Orlando*, you see! Virginia's amusement at playing with my mother in this way, my mother's amusement at being played with. And of course they made no attempt to conceal it in the first edition. There are photographs taken in the garden or fields around Longbarn of my mother with her dogs. And in the next room we've got the portrait of Shelmerdine.[8] It's in my father's diary that Virginia and my mother went together to Knole to choose the illustrations for this book which my mother hadn't read.[9] But she *loved* it!

So that was my mother's reaction to *Orlando*. And that's my feeling about it. Do I feel I'm 'reading my mother's biography'? Well, obviously it isn't. Oh, some of the details are accurate, but it's a fantasy. It's a fantastic picture of my mother.

NOTES

Nigel Nicolson (b. 1917), writer and politician, co-founder of Weidenfeld & Nicolson, Publishers. Nicolson served as Conservative MP for Bournemouth East from 1952 to 1959. Author of several books on architecture, politics and social history, he edited his father's diaries and co-edited the six-volume edition of *The Letters of Virginia Woolf*.

1. At Sissinghurst Castle, Kent, the home of Nicolson's parents, Sir Harold Nicolson and Vita Sackville-West.
2. Charles Raymond Bell Mortimer (1895–1980), journalist and art critic.
3. The Nicolsons' home before 1930.
4. Published by the Hogarth Press in May 1930.
5. The history of Sackville-West's family, the book had just been published (*Letters*, II, 600–1).

6. That is, the Henry W. and Albert A. Berg Collection of English
and American Literature at the New York Public Library.
7. Published in the *Listener*, 27 January 1955.
8. Marmaduke Bonthrop Shelmerdine, Orlando's husband.
9. See below.

About Virginia*

VITA SACKVILLE-WEST and SIR HAROLD NICOLSON

Vita Sackville-West to Harold Nicolson

28th October, 1927. Long Barn.   I have had Virginia here all day,
and she has just gone. We had fun this morning. We went up to
Knole and chose pictures for *Orlando*. We chose obscure pictures,
out of which we will take bits. That book sounds more fantastic
the more I hear of it!

Harold Nicolson's Diary

4th May, 1931.   Go with Leonard and Virginia Woolf to see the
French talking-film, *Le Million*.[1] The theatre is crowded with intellectuals, from which it is evident that this form of intelligent
talkie has a great future before it. The French talent for amusing
dialogue finds an enormous scope in this rapid motion and will
render American films completely old-fashioned.

Harold Nicolson's Diary

14th August, 1932.   We ... go off to Rodmell to visit Leonard
and Virginia Woolf. V. is ill, and takes my V. up to her room.
Talk to Leonard about my Peace Conference book.[2] Look at the

* From *Diaries and Letters 1930–1939*, ed. Nigel Nicolson (London: Collins;
New York: Atheneum, 1966) pp. 32, 72, 121, 188, 350–1, and *Diaries and Letters
1939–1945*, ed. Nigel Nicolson (London: Collins; New York: Atheneum, 1967)
pp. 146–7, 157–9.

garden. Their sky is as wide and clear as the sky above the downs. We come back to Rottingdean feeling as usual lightened and inspired.

Vita Sackville-West to Harold Nicolson

9th November, 1934. Sissinghurst.   In London yesterday I went to try on my new clothes at Jay's. . . . Then I went to luncheon with Virginia, who gave me an imitation of Yeats telling her why he was occult.[3] He has been confirmed in this theory because he saw a coat-hanger emerge from his cupboard and travel across the foot of his bed; next night, it emerged again, clothed in one of his jackets; the third night, a hand emerged from one of the cuffs; the fourth night – 'Ah! Mrs Woolf, that would be a long story; enough to say, I finally recovered my potency'.

Vita Sackville-West to Harold Nicolson

3rd August, 1938. Sissinghurst.   I went to Rodmell for last night, and very nice it was too. We sat out in the garden watching the late sunlight making the corn all golden over the Downs. Then I had a long talk this morning with Virginia, who was in her most delightful mood. Tell your host, if you think it would please him, that Virginia much admired his autobiography (*The Summing Up*).[4] She had liked the clarity of his style, and also the honesty with which he tried to get at the truth. She liked the analysis of his own methods of writing.

Oh my dear, what an enchanting person Virginia is! How she weaves magic into life! Whenever I see her, she raises life to a higher level. How cheap she makes people like——seem! And Leonard too: with his schoolboyish love for pets and toys (gadgets), he is irresistibly young and attractive. How wrong people are about Bloomsbury, saying that it is devitalised and devitalising. You couldn't find two people less devitalised or devitalising than the Wolves – or indeed people more vitalising than Roger Fry, for example. I think that where Bloomsbury has suffered is in its hangers-on like——and equivalent young men, and of course the drooping Lytton must have done its cause a great deal of harm. I hated Lytton.

Vita Sackville-West to Harold Nicolson

18th February, 1941. Monk's House, Rodmell.   Virginia has gone to
talk to the servants, and I sit alone in her friendly room with its
incredible muddle of objects, so crowded that I am terrified of
knocking something over. I've already broken a chair. Leonard
has departed for the market, laden with baskets of apples and
carrots. They *are* nice. Leonard has now got a cat, which means
that the rooms are further crowded by tin dishes on the floor.

Vita Sackville-West to Harold Nicolson

31st March, 1941. Sissinghurst.   I have just had the most awful
shock: Virginia has killed herself. It is not in the papers, but I got
letters from Leonard and also from Vanessa telling me. It was
last Friday. Leonard came home to find a note saying that she
was going to commit suicide, and they think she had drowned
herself, as he found her stick floating on the river. He says she
had not been well for the last few weeks and was terrified of
going mad again. He says, 'It was, I suppose, the strain of the
war and finishing her book,[5] and she could not rest or eat'.
    I simply can't take it in. That lovely mind, that lovely spirit.
And she seemed so well when I last saw her, and I had a jokey
letter from her only a couple of weeks ago.[6] She must have been
quite out of her mind or she would never have brought such
sorrow and horror on Leonard. Vanessa had seen him and says
he was amazingly self-controlled and calm, but insisted on being
left alone.

Harold Nicolson to Vita Sackville-West

3rd April, 1941. Ministry of Information.   Of course I came down
because of Virginia. But I saw no reason to mention the thing.
There was nothing that could be said. I just wanted to be with
you. I hate it so. It is horrible to see her picture in the papers.
My heart absolutely aches with sympathy for Leonard.

Vita Sackville-West to Harold Nicolson

8th April, 1941. I went to see Vanessa yesterday at Charleston. She could not have been nicer and told me all about it. Rather to my dismay, she said that Leonard wanted to see me. So I went to Monk's House. He was having his tea – just one tea-cup on the table where they always had tea. The house was full of his flowers, and all Virginia's things lying about as usual. He said, 'Let us go somewhere more comfortable', and took me up to her sitting-room. There was her needle-work on a chair and all her coloured wools hanging over a sort of little towel-horse which she had had made for them. Her thimble on the table. Her scribbling block with her writing on it. The window from which one can see the river.

I said, 'Leonard, I do not like your being here alone like this'. He turned those piercing blue eyes on me and said, 'It is the only thing to do'. I saw then that he was right. But it must take some courage.

He talked about the whole thing perfectly calmly and in great detail, shirking nothing. Some phrases bit. He said, 'When we couldn't find her anywhere, I went up to a derelict house which she was fond of in the Downs, called Mad Misery, but she wasn't there'. I remember her telling me about Mad Misery and saying that she would take me there one day. They have been dragging the river, but are now giving up the search. As the river is tidal, she has probably been carried out to sea. I hope so. I hope they will never find her.

She could swim. I knew this because of a story she once told me about Rupert Brooke at Cambridge, when they were both very young, and he took off all his clothes and plunged naked into a moonlit pool, and she thought she must do likewise; so she did, although very shy, and they swam about together. But it appears that when she went to drown herself, she was wearing big gumboots (which she seldom did because she hated them), and if those had filled with water, they would have dragged her down. Also she may have weighted her pockets with stones. The river is banked up with stones. The only thing that puzzles them is that they never found her hat floating. But Vanessa thinks it had an elastic to keep it on, so went down with her.

NOTES

For information about Vita Sackville-West, see p. 36.

Harold George Nicolson (1886–1968; baronet), career diplomat, writer and parliamentarian, was active in literary circles and devoted his later career to writing.

   1. Directed by René Clair.
   2. *Peacemaking* (1933) on the Paris Peace Conference of 1919, which Nicolson had attended.
   3. William Butler Yeats (1865–1939), Irish poet and playwright.
   4. Nicolson was at Cap Ferrat, France, visiting W. Somerset Maugham (1874–1965), novelist, short-story writer and dramatist.
   5. *Between the Acts*.
   6. Sackville-West's last meeting with Woolf occurred on 18 February 1941. Woolf's last letter to Sackville-West was written on [22 March 1941] (see *Letters*, VI, 484).

Part IV
Bloomsbury

Virginia and her Set*

GERALD BRENAN

The set I moved in, which centred round that small group of older people later known as the 'Bloomsbury Group', had certain things in common. They had all of them been at either Oxford or Cambridge, they were much better off than I was and they had none of them fought in the war. Some had been medically unfit, others pacifists, one had served in the Red Cross, others were too young to have been called up.[1] For many years I met no one except Ralph [Partridge] who had been at the front. Not only did the war seem to have been entirely forgotten, but those who had fought in it were slightly looked down on as people who had taken part in a shabby and barbarous enterprise. I on the other hand was proud of having been through it and felt that there was something thin and unreal about those who had not done so. They had missed the great experience of the age and that, I said to myself when I was in a priggish mood, was one of the reasons for their futility. Their comfortable incomes, their cliquishness, their suspicion of new adventures in literature, their lack of any connections with the larger world made me feel that, much as I liked and admired many of them, it would not do for me as a writer to get too involved with them. I wanted to have my own life, not to move in a small literary set or to become anyone's disciple. Yet, bound to Carrington as I was, I was becoming partly absorbed by them.

The ones among them I most admired were Leonard and Virginia Woolf. I was seeing them fairly often that summer so I will quote two extracts from my letter to Carrington that relate to them. The first is dated May 6th, 1924.

* From *Personal Record: 1920–1972* (London: Jonathan Cape, 1974; New York: Knopf, 1975) pp. 78–9, 155–7 and *South from Granada* (London: Hamish Hamilton; New York: Farrar, Straus and Cudahy, 1957) pp. 143–6.

I saw Virginia last night, sitting in her dressing gown and looking rather ruffled and stormtossed, like a bird that has just crossed the sea in a gale. She was very nice and asked me to come to her parties in the evenings. I said I would like to come if I need not talk. 'But really, Gerald, you know you are a perfect chatterbox'. I walked round the square with Leonard and came home and read for *Teresa*.[2]

Now I will quote from my second letter, dated June 3rd.

I went to see Virginia. Mrs Joad[3] (who acted as their secretary) was there and Adrian Stephen and George Sanger. Leonard now takes pleasure in putting me through various tests as though I were some new and quaint form of animal. When he opened the street door he quickly stepped behind it. But I saw him and asked him why he did that. 'To see what you would do', he said. I see now that his treatment of me and possibly of all new people consists in a series of elaborately arranged tests or experiments, from each of which he draws some conclusion. No doubt he arranges them in a kind of series, like those keys for discovering the names of flowers at the beginning of botany books: one is sifted from genus to sub-genus, and as each experiment is supposed to be conclusive and irrevocable, the result is at last a pure fantasy. Far from resenting this, I find it gives me pleasure. Leonard's unflattering remarks could offend nobody, and every time I see him I like him better.

When you told me that he liked cactuses, you threw a great deal of light on his character, for what interests him in men is what they share with these plants – variety, quaintness, hard-cut outlines, immobility.

Virginia was discussing her favourite subject – the difference between the younger and the older generations. 'Look at Gerald...', she began. 'Gerald', said Leonard, 'is completely disoriented – he lives upside down on his head'. Though I did not agree, I thought I could guess what he meant, but he went on, 'All the younger generation are like him. Marjorie (Mrs Joad) is just the same. They are all disoriented'. And then I understood nothing. For that the quality (invisible to me) which I have in common with Mrs Joad and Ralph and many others should be called 'disorientation' was quite incomprehensible.

'They are less subtle, less sensitive, but more downright and more intelligent', went on Virginia. 'As for intelligence', said Leonard, 'I would back myself against all of them'.

Leonard, I thought to myself, will always be, wherever he is, the most intelligent person in the room, even when Roger Fry or Bertie Russell[4] are present. And this is because, having a head so clear that no one could have a clearer, he has energy to spare for watching and comparing the speakers and their psychological motives: that is to say, he is detached and this gives him a feeling of superiority, of being in some sense more intelligent than even people like B. R. [Bertrand Russell], whose mental capacity he sums up under the rather disparaging word 'brilliant'.

* * *

My diary does not give much space to Bloomsbury parties or conversaziones, but here is a brief account of one which I will quote:

Jan 28.   At 10 a small party at Angus Davidson's for conversation.[5] Virginia, Vanessa, Julia Strachey, Mme Raverat,[6] Edith Sitwell and one foreigner: the rest men, for it is not easy to put women in a room with the Stephen sisters. Lytton and his young man Philip Ritchie, Leonard Woolf, Duncan Grant, James and Oliver Strachey, Raymond Mortimer and one or two others. It was amusing. Virginia leaning stiffly sideways attacked the painters: how fantastic they were, how only the smallest details interested them, how they argued about everything. Vanessa and Duncan will talk for an hour on end simply on a cat. 'Only three legs!' 'Yes, and a white spot on its tail'. 'I'm sure I don't know how it catches mice. 'But it doesn't'. 'Oh, but I've seen it'. 'You're quite wrong about that, Duncan!'

Wherever Virginia goes she undoes a knot like a Lapland witch and lets out a war: an old well-practised war, whose tactics have been polished up by many previous encounters. If it is not the Older Generation v. the Younger, it is Writers v. Painters or even Men v. Women. It is these well-worn topics that produce the most brilliant and fantastic conversation that one can hear anywhere in England. . . .

I was always divided in my loyalty to 'Bloomsbury', considered as a group. There could be no doubt about the high level of their intelligence, while their cult of good conversation made them very stimulating people to know. But I thought that Maynard Keynes' description of them as 'water spiders swimming gracefully on the surface of the stream' contained a good deal of truth.[7] Civilized, liberal, agnostic or atheist like their parents before them, they had always stood too far above the life of their day, had been too little exposed to its rough-and-tumble really to belong to it. Thus, though they thought of themselves as new brooms and innovators, they quickly found they were playing the part of a literary establishment. What I chiefly got from them was their respect for the truth. Yet this – they gave the word a capital letter – was defined in a narrow and exclusive way so that anyone who held views that could not be justified rationally was regarded as a wilful cultivator of illusions and therefore as a person who could not be taken seriously. Religion in particular was anathema. The subject was finished, closed, or existed merely as a personal weakness or as a hangover from early associations, like not washing or continuing to play with dolls or tin soldiers. That psychological pressures could drive people to believe things that could not be proved rationally or scientifically was something that they refused to allow. Scepticism was a moral duty. They thus found themselves out of touch both with large areas of the world they lived in and with most of the past. For if history showed, as they thought, a slow progress from superstition to enlightenment, why bother to understand the impulses that drove people to religious belief, much less to Communism or Nazism? By saying 'they're so stupid', they imagined that they had disposed of them.

This attitude was illustrated for me by their opinion of Joyce's *Ulysses*. Lytton dismissed it by saying that he could not find a single intelligent sentence in it. Virginia was more hesitant, yet disliked it for being vulgar and lower class. Morgan Forster attacked it as a book that covered the universe with filth and mud. Not one of my friends, except Arthur Waley, had a good word to say for it. Yet for me Joyce was, after Proust, the greatest novelist of the century and their incapacity to see any merit in him showed how conventional their minds were. They lived by good taste and I saw with regret that I was being carried along the same road and being obliged to live by it too.

What I also found lacking in these élite circles was the range and variety of human types which a painter or writer rubs shoulders with in a Bohemian or merely more open world. They all smelt of the University. They had been brain-washed and class-conditioned there.

* * *

To appreciate Virginia Woolf's brilliance as a talker one had to see her in her own circle of friends. It was a regular custom for five or six of these to meet every week after dinner either at her house or at her sister Vanessa's, and usually one or two of the younger generation would be invited to be present. In that capacity I went several times. The aces were Roger Fry, Duncan Grant, Vanessa Bell, Clive Bell, Lytton Strachey, Maynard Keynes, and occasionally one or two people such as Desmond MacCarthy and Morgan Forster who did not, I think, regard themselves as 'belonging to Bloomsbury', though they were accepted by the others on the same footing. The arrangements were informal, yet everyone was aware of the purpose of the meeting, which was to make good conversation. With this idea, for literary people at this time were very sober, no drinks except coffee were provided.

I very soon got the impression that these conversaziones were really of the nature of orchestral concerts. One might almost say that the score was provided, for the same themes always came up – the difference between the younger and the older generation, the difference between the painter and the writer, and so forth. The performers too were thoroughly practised, for they had been meeting every week or even more often over a space of many years to discuss the same not, one would have thought, very inspiring subjects. Thus they had each of them learned what part he must play to conduce to the best general effect and also how to stimulate and give the cue for the others. The solo instruments, one might say (both strings), were Virginia Woolf and Duncan Grant: they could be relied on to produce at the appropriate moment some piece of elaborate fantasy, contradicting the serious and persistent assertions of the other instruments. Roger Fry would drive forward on one of his provocative lines: Vanessa Bell, the most silent of the company, would drop one of her *mots*, while Clive Bell, fulfilling the role of the bassoon, would keep up a general roar of animation. His special function in the performance was to egg on and provoke Virginia to one of her famous sallies.

What one got from these evenings was, if my youthful judgement

is to be relied on, conversation of a brilliance and (in spite of the
rehearsals) spontaneity which, I imagine, has rarely been heard
in England before. I have known other good talkers, one of them
perhaps the equal of any of these, but they have always given
solo performances. What 'Bloomsbury' evenings offered was the
concert in which each talked to produce himself and to draw the
best out of the others. I imagine that only continual practice by
people who share the same general attitude to life and who are
as pleased by their friends' performance as by their own can provide
anything like it.

For a young writer even a slight acquaintance with such a group
of people was an education, though not perhaps a stimulus. They
had standards – honesty, intelligence, taste, devotion to the arts,
and social sophistication. They never, in their written judgements,
let their vanity or their private friendships or their political or
religious prejudices run away with them, and they were none of
them out to compensate for their own weaknesses and deficiencies
by attacking others. Yet it must, I think, be admitted that they
lived – not singly, which would not have mattered, but collec-
tively – in an ivory tower. Maynard Keynes and Leonard Woolf
had roots outside it in the world of politics, and Roger Fry was
too active and public spirited a man to let himself be confined.
The others, however were prisoners of their close web of mutual
friendships and of their agreeable mode of life and also of their
rather narrow and (as they held it) smug Cambridge philosophy.
Virginia Woolf, it is true, was always aware of the typist queu-
ing for her lunch in the cheap tea-shop and of the shabby old
lady weeping in the third-class railway carriage, yet she too was
tied to her set by her birth, her social proclivities, her craving for
praise and flattery, and could only throw distant and uneasy glances
outside it. Her sense of the precariousness of things, which gives
her work its seriousness, came from her private life – from the
shock of her brother Thoby's death and from her experience of
madness. But the ethos of her group and indeed her whole cultured Victorian upbringing cut her off from the hard view of human
nature that the novelist needs and drove her to develop her own
poetic and mystical vision of things in what I at least feel was
too subjective a way. Thus when one re-reads her novels now
one feels again the ease and beauty of much of the writing and
gets a certain muffled, Calderon-like impression of life being no
more than a dream,[8] yet one is left dissatisfied. For if one is to be

convinced that life is a dream, one must first be shown, and pretty sharply, that what is set before one is life.

Looking back today it is not, I think, difficult to see that the weakness inherent in the splendid flower of English culture thrown up by 'Bloomsbury' lay in its being so closely attached to a class and mode of life that was dying. Already by 1930 it was pot-bound. Its members were too secure, too happy, too triumphant, too certain of the superiority of their Parnassian philosophy to be able to draw fresh energies from the new and disturbing era that was coming in. They had escaped the shock of the first German war . . . and had not taken warning from the prophets who announced that the snug rationalist world they lived in was seriously threatened. When they should, therefore, have been in their prime, they were on their way to being an anachronism, even Virginia Woolf – the most open-minded of all except Maynard Keynes – being limited by some deep-seated doubt (connected possibly with her fits of madness) about the reality of almost everything except literature. Yet, I imagine, if the cobalt bomb does not obliterate everything, future ages will feel an interest in these people because they stand for something that the world always looks on with nostalgia – an *ancien régime*. They carried the arts of civilized life and friendship to a very high point, and their work reflects this civilization. Then, surely, two of them at least, Virginia Woolf and Maynard Keynes, possessed those rare imaginative gifts that are known as genius.

NOTES

For information about Gerald Brenan, see p. 50.

1. Leonard Woolf and Lytton Strachey received medical exemptions. Duncan Grant and David Garnett were pacifists. E. M. Forster served with the Red Cross in Alexandria.
2. That is, Teresa of Avila (1515–82), Spanish mystic.
3. Marjorie Thomson 'Joad', companion of the philosopher C. E. M. Joad, was an early partner of the Hogarth Press.
4. Bertrand Arthur William Russell (1872–1970; 3rd Earl Russell), philosopher, social commentator and writer on diverse topics.
5. Angus Henry Gordon Davidson (1898–1980), translator and biographer.
6. Gwendolyn Mary Raverat, née Darwin (1885–1957), wood-engraver.
7. Cf. 'I can see us as water-spiders, gracefully skimming, as light and reasonable as air, the surface of the stream', 'My Early Beliefs'

(1938), *Essays in Biography*, vol. X of *The Collected Writings of John Maynard Keynes* (London: Macmillan, 1972) p. 450. John Maynard Keynes (1883–1946; peerage 1942), economist and influential economic theorist.

8. Echo of the title *La vida es sueño* (1635) by Pedro Calderón de la Barca.

'Electricity in the air'*

FRANCES PARTRIDGE

[Alix Strachey][1] was the only one of the many who worked at the Hogarth Press who stayed exactly one day. 'Leonard and Virginia were very kind', she told me. 'They said they would leave me to get used to the press while they went for a walk. It was quite *incredibly* boring. I said to myself, "I can't possibly spend the rest of my life doing this", and when they came back I told them so. They took it very well, I must say'.

I do not feel I can add anything to all that has been written about the Woolves. Brilliant as she was, I found Virginia less lovable than her sister Vanessa, whose passion for colour she emulated in words. I think perhaps she was really a little jealous of Vanessa for actually having the power to squeeze her colours from a tube on to the canvas. Both the sisters were apparently unself-conscious about their remarkable beauty, but their two faces reflected an essential difference of character. Virginia's bore the stigmata that are to be seen in many who have been gravely mad – a subtly agonised tautness, something twisted; the way she held herself, turned her head or smoked a cigarette struck one as awkward even while it charmed and interested one. As Julia Strachey said of her, she 'was not at home in her body'. The lines of Vanessa's beautiful face had been graven by human emotions, and responses to other people, with the traces also of her unexpected bursts of hilarity and recklessness. She was famous for her mixed metaphors (like 'the longest worm has its turning' and 'in that house one meets a dark horse in every cupboard') and she could be

* From *Memories* (London: Gollancz, 1981) pp. 79–81.

delightfully witty too. As she got old and moved more slowly, it was as if one of the statues from the Acropolis had stepped down from her pedestal and was taking a stately walk.

In Virginia's house there was always electricity in the air, and though enthralled by the display of lightning, few people were entirely at their ease there, or could fail to wonder where the next flash would strike. She seemed at her best with Clive Bell, of whom she was genuinely fond, and who would act as midwife to her verbal fantasies with a gentle 'Ye-e-e-es, Virginia?' But then Clive was a born host, with the rare gift of wanting his guests to shine rather than trying to do so himself.

NOTES

Frances Catherine Partridge, née Marshall (b. 1900), translator and diarist. She became acquainted with Bloomsbury as the second wife of Ralph Partridge and as an employee in David Garnett's bookshop.

1. Alix Strachey, née Sargant Florence (1892–1973), psychoanalyst, who with her husband James (Lytton Strachey's brother) promulgated Freud's theories in England.

'A genius who worked magic'*

CLIVE BELL

That I should have been amongst the first, perhaps the very first, to write a full dress article on Virginia Woolf is neither surprising nor important. I believe it was published in America, possibly in *Vanity Fair* under Frank Crowninshield's rule; but I am not sure. Because I should like to be sure, I mention the matter at the very beginning of this chapter. I should like to know to whom I ought to apologise for making free with his or her property. I have lost track of the thing; and all I can discover is a dirty

* 'Virginia Woolf', *Old Friends: Personal Recollections* (London: Chatto & Windus, 1956; New York: Harcourt, Brace, 1957) pp. 92–118.

manuscript written presumably in 1922 or 23 since it ends with
an elaborate criticism of *Jacob's Room*, described as 'Mrs Woolf's
latest novel'.[1] For the rest, it is a longish piece of five thousand
words or so, but was I dare say cut down for publication. I should
be amused to see how it looks in print, though I cannot say that
in manuscript it reads particularly well: maybe at the time it seemed
interesting because so little was known of the subject. Be that as
it may, I shall not hesitate to make use of this manuscript if any
bit seems worth saving; and perhaps the criticism is not worthless after all, for I do remember that when, some years later, a
French writer produced an appreciation, his victim was amiable
enough to tell me that it was a poor thing of which the best part
was a paraphrase of what I had already published. Naturally I
remember the compliment, but now, looking at it suspiciously, I
cannot quite decide from which hand it comes.

As I was saying, that I should have been one of the first to
sing the praises of Virginia Woolf is not surprising. I had known
her since she was a girl of twenty, and in the years between my
marriage to her sister in 1907 and her marriage to Leonard Woolf
in 1912 I was to some extent her literary confidant. From earliest
days I admired her reviews in *The Times Literary Supplement, The
Cornhill* and *The Guardian*, and perhaps that was why she took
me into her confidence and showed me short imaginative pieces
few, if any, of which have been printed. Why should they have
been? To me they were thrilling because they revealed – so I
thought and thought rightly – in a person I cared for, genius; but
to a coldly critical eye perhaps they would have seemed no more
than a gifted girl practising. During these years we met regularly, once a week I dare say, to talk about writing generally and
her writing in particular; with pleasure I remember that already
I possessed sufficient sense of proportion to say nothing about
mine. And yet we contrived to quarrel occasionally: we were both
young. I call to mind some famous rows: and I have by me a
picture post-card from Siena, written many years later, with an
inky cross against a spot on the fortezza and beneath this legend
– 'Here Clive quarrelled with his sister-in-law'.

However, it is neither about our bookish talks nor yet about
her books that I want to say my word, though doubtless I shall
have said something about the latter before I have done. What I
want to do is something much more difficult. I want to give an
idea, an adumbration, of the most remarkable person I have known

intimately. I cannot hope perfectly to succeed; the task is beyond my powers, and would, I fancy, be beyond the powers of any writer unless he were an artist possessing gifts comparable with those of his subject. Yet for a professional critic who has known and known well a genius – a genius who worked magic not only in art but in life; for such a critic, so fortunately placed, to despair of giving any account of the impression made on him, would be in my opinion poor-spirited. I will do my best. Two people I have known from whom emanated simply and unmistakably a sense of genius: the other is Picasso.[2] With Picasso I have been acquainted for fifty years almost, and at one time I saw a good deal of him; but I do not pretend to have known him well. Picasso I would not attempt to describe, though later I may have some tales to tell about him. Nevertheless, had I never seen a picture by Picasso I should have been aware of his genius: I knew him well enough for that. Similarly, had I never read a book by Virginia I should have been aware of hers. It has been my fortune to be friends with a number of very clever people: Maynard Keynes, the cleverest man I ever met, Roger Fry, Lytton Strachey, Raymond Mortimer, Jean Cocteau. None of them cast the peculiar spell I am trying to characterise. The difference between these very clever people and the less clever, between Roger Fry and me for instance, was it seemed one of degree rather than kind. There was no reason in nature why I should not have been as bright as Roger, only I happened not to be. I can imagine myself as bright as Roger; I cannot imagine myself in the least like Virginia or Picasso. With Roger's understanding and mental processes mine were of a kind: I thought and reasoned and invented and arrived at conclusions as he did, only I thought and reasoned and invented less well. But Virginia and Picasso belonged to another order of beings; they were of a species distinct from the common; their mental processes were different from ours; they arrived at conclusions by ways to us unknown. Also those conclusions or comments or judgments or flights of fancy or witticisms, or little jokes even, were true or convincing or effective or delightful for reasons that are not the reasons of logic nor yet of our well tried commonsense. Their standards, too, were of their own creation: yet spontaneously we appraised by those standards, which for the moment we not only accepted but appropriated, whatever they chose to offer. Their conclusions were as satisfying as the conclusions of mathematics though reached by quite other roads; for though they might seem to have postulated that two and two made five their answers always came out right. All this is clumsy and perhaps beside the point. The point is that half an hour's conversation with Virginia sufficed to make one realise that she had genius.

I want in this attempt to describe Virginia to dispel certain false notions. One result of the publication of extracts from her diary (*A Writer's Diary*, Hogarth Press) has been to confirm an opinion already current, the opinion that Virginia's nature was harsh and unhappy. Nothing could be further from the truth. Yet, though the inference drawn from the published diaries is false it would be excusable had not the editor, Mr Leonard Woolf, been at pains to put readers on their guard. On the very first page of his preface he writes: 'At the best and even unexpurgated, diaries give a distorted or one-sided portrait of the writer, because, as Virginia Woolf herself remarks somewhere in these diaries, one gets into the habit of recording one particular kind of mood – irritation or misery, say – and of not writing one's diary when one is feeling the opposite. The portrait is therefore from the start unbalanced, and, if someone then deliberately removes another characteristic, it may well become a mere caricature'.[3]

Someone did remove another characteristic. The editor, himself, very properly cut out a number of passages which were much too personal, not to say libellous, to be published while the victims were alive.

Despite this warning, there are those who find confirmation in these diaries of what they wish to believe and retell the old tale – Virginia Woolf was gloomy and querulous; so I will add a few sentences to what her husband has said clearly enough. More often than not the diary was written in moments of agitation, depression or nervous irritation; also the published extracts are concerned almost entirely with her work, a subject about which she never felt calmly. Indeed, creating a work of art, as the diary shows, was for Virginia a cause, not only of moral but of physical exasperation – exasperation so intense that often it made her positively ill. I should not be surprised if some lively journalist had dubbed the book 'Screams from the torture-chamber', for truly much of it must have been written when the author felt much as one feels at the worst moments of tooth-ache. Even so, were the unpublished part (the published is not a twentieth of the whole) before the reader, it is certain that his idea of the writer would change completely. Of this unpublished part I know only scraps;

and even these will not be printed for some years I surmise. Nor can I choose but rejoice; for amongst pages of gay and brilliant description will be found many disobliging comments on the sayings and doings and characters of her friends – of whom I was one. Wherefore here and now I should like to interpose a caution. Those comments and descriptions, those that I have read or heard read, though always lively and amusing are not always true.

Sooner or later Virginia's diaries and letters will be printed. They will make a number of fascinating volumes; books, like Byron's letters, to be read and re-read for sheer delight. In the midst of his delight let the reader remember, especially the reader who itches to compose histories and biographies, that the author's accounts of people and of their sayings and goings may be flights of her airy imagination. Well do I remember an evening when Leonard Woolf, reading aloud to a few old friends extracts from these diaries, stopped suddenly. 'I suspect', said I, 'you've come on a passage where she makes a bit too free with the frailties and absurdities of someone here present'. 'Yes', said he, 'but that's not why I broke off. I shall skip the next few pages because there's not a word of truth in them'.

That Virginia possessed the poet's, and dreamer's, faculty of 'making Cables of Cobwebbes and Wildernesses of handsome Groves' will surprise no one who has read her books; what may surprise is that she should have employed this faculty not in art but in life. I have gone so far as to conjecture – and it was going rather far I admit – that at times she saw life and to some extent experienced it as a novel or rather as a series of novels, in which anyone of her friends might find him or herself cast, all unawares, for a part. Yours might be sympathetic role, and in that case all you said and did would be seen through roseate lenses, your banal comments would be transmuted to words of wisdom or subtle intuition, your ungainly gestures would acquire an air of dignity and significance. Sometimes, however – in my case generally – it was quite the other way. But for better or for worse one's character, conduct and conversation had to fit in to a picture which existed in the artist's imagination. To one's surprise, often to one's dismay, one found oneself the embodiment of a preconceived idea.

I felt so sure that there was something in my theory that I propounded it to one of Virginia's friends, from whom I heard a story to confirm my suspicions. This friend happened to be a

lady, elegant and aristocratic to be sure, but unconventional to
the verge of eccentricity.[4] Her manners certainly were all that
manners should be; but she was a rebel at heart, and her conversation and way of life would have shocked her mother profoundly
and did shock her more sedate relations. No one could have been
less like a leader of Victorian society. Nevertheless, in one of those
marvellous romances which were a part of Virginia's everyday
existence, that is what this wayward individual – Lady X shall
we call her? – had to be: the typical leader of rather old-fashioned
'Society', exquisite and soignée (as she was) but also classically
correct, smooth and sure of herself, running true to form in a
world of dukes, ambassadors and orchids. To give a sharper point
to this imaginary relationship – the friendship of a *grande dame*
and a novelist – Virginia, who besides being one of the most
beautiful was one of the best bred women of her age, cast herself
in the role of a tough, uncouth, out-at-elbows Bohemian – of genius.
And such was the spell she threw, such the cogency of her imagination, that many a time poor Lady X found herself, not only playing
up to the role assigned to her, but positively accepting Virginia
in the role she had allotted to herself. Am I not justified, then, in
beseeching a vast posterity of enchanted readers to be on their
guard?

To return for a moment to that silly caricature – Virginia the gloomy
malcontent – let me say once and for all that she was about the
gayest human being I have known and one of the most lovable. I
was going to add 'besides being a genius'; but indeed these qualities
were elements of her genius: in that sense she was all of a piece.
I am not suggesting that she was faultless, or that those who
have suspected her of being a little jealous on occasions or un-
willing to 'brook a rival near the throne' were merely malevolent
gossips. Only her jealousies and lapses of sympathy were of such
a peculiar kind that it is difficult to understand them and easy to
exaggerate. I do not pretend to understand them entirely, and so
will give an example or two, leaving the reader to provide his
own explanation. Someone said in her presence that it must be
very tiring for her sister, a painter, to stand long hours at the
easel. Virginia, outraged, I suppose, by the insinuation that her
sister's occupation was in any way more exacting than her own,
went out at once and bought a tall desk at which she insisted on

standing to write. But this was when she was very young, and the very young are apt to be touchy. Surely she was guilty of excessive touchiness when she complained – a friend having told her I had said in a letter that she was looking well (she had been ill) – that 'Clive thinks I have become red and coarse'. It was a sort of jealousy, no doubt, that made her deprecate her friends pursuing the arts or professions which seemed in some way to put them in competition with herself. From time to time she would regret that Duncan Grant had not accepted a commission in the Black Watch – 'I feel sure he would have been a remarkable soldier' (so do I). I believe she herself felt that she had gone a little far when she told me that Lytton Strachey should have been an Indian civil servant; but perhaps she was right when she persuaded Molly MacCarthy[5] to write me a letter (to which I replied beginning 'Dearest Virginia') pointing out that critics were mere parasites on art and that my abilities (such as they were) would be much better employed at the Bar. I think there was a sort of jealousy in all this, but I also think there was a sort, a very odd sort, of Victorianism. Sometimes it seemed to me that Virginia had inherited from her immediate ancestors more than their beauty and intelligence. Every good Victorian knew that a young man should have a sensible profession, something solid and secure, which would lead naturally to a comfortable old age and a fair provision for the children. In her head Virginia knew perfectly well that to give such advice to Lytton or Duncan was absurd; but Virginia, like the merest man, was not always guided by reason.

I said 'the merest man' because Virginia was, in her peculiar way, an ardent feminist. What is more, some of her injustices and wanton denigrations can be traced, I think, to female indignation. In political feminism – the Suffrage Movement – she was not much interested, though I do remember that once or twice she and I went to some obscure office where we licked up envelopes for the Adult Suffrage League. But, as you will have guessed, it was not in political action that her feminism expressed itself: indeed she made merciless fun of the flag-wagging fanaticism of her old friend Ethel Smyth. What she minded most, perhaps, was what she considered male advantages, and especially advantages in education. Readers of *A Room of One's Own* will remember an amusing, but none the less bitter, comparison of lunch in King's with dinner at Girton; and intelligent readers will have felt that

the comparison is to be carried a great deal further. Also she
resented the way in which men, as she thought, patronised women,
especially women who were attempting to create works of art or
succeed in what were once considered manly professions. Assur-
edly Virginia did not wish to be a man, or to be treated as a
man: she wished to be treated as an equal – just possibly as a
superior. Anyhow the least suspicion of condescension irritated
her intensely and understandably. She grew angry and lashed
out; and her blows fell, as often as not, on innocent noses. She
could be monstrously, but delightfully, unfair; and witty blows
below the belt sometimes leave nasty bruises. Neither male nor
female can be wholly objective about *Three Guineas*; but for my
part I feel sure it is her least admirable production.

Virginia's feminism was genuine and ardent, yet I do not think
it played a great part in her life. Certainly the tantrums to which
it gave rise were rare and transitory; and I will make bold, and
bold it is, to say that hers was a happy nature. I know all about
those fits of black despair; she had something to be desperate
about, seeing that always hung over her the threat of collapse if
she indulged too freely her ruling passion – the passion to create.
Writing was her passion and her joy and her poison. Yet, I repeat,
hers was a happy nature and she was happy. As for her gaiety –
does this seem significant? My children, from the time they were
old enough to enjoy anything beyond their animal satisfactions,
enjoyed beyond anything a visit from Virginia. They looked forward to it as the greatest treat imaginable: 'Virginia's coming,
what fun we shall have'. That is what they said and felt when
they were children and went on saying and feeling to the end.
And so said all of us. So said everyone who knew her. 'What fun
we shall have' and what fun we did have. She might be divinely
witty or outrageously fanciful; she might retail village gossip or
tell stories of her London friends; always she was indescribably
entertaining; always she enjoyed herself and we enjoyed her. 'Virginia's coming to tea': we knew it would be exciting, we knew
that we were going to laugh and be surprised and made to feel
that the temperature of life was several degrees higher than we
had supposed.

I have not yet said what I want to say, I have not succeeded in
giving an idea of Virginia's high spirits and lovable nature, so let
me try another method. Barbara Bagenal[6] was a girl of whom
Virginia was fond; but Barbara Bagenal would be the last to claim

that she was one of Virginia's closest friends. However, Barbara was down on her luck: she had been looking forward to a grand holiday, six weeks in Spain, and a day or two before she was to start she had been struck down by scarlet fever. That was a disaster with the misery of which Virginia could sympathise, and she showed her sympathy to some purpose. To her unhappy friend in hospital she wrote, and wrote precisely the sort of letters anyone in hospital would like to receive. The nurses insisted on burning most of them, but here is one that escaped.

Hogarth House. 24th June 1923

My dear Barbara,

I should have written to you before, but I have had so many disasters lately from writing letters, that nothing short of death or bankruptcy will in future draw one from me. I hope scarlet fever isn't about as bad as going bankrupt. I have often thought of you in your hospital, as I take my way about the streets in comparative freedom. Yet I would have changed places with you last Sunday fortnight, when Ottoline completely drew the veils of illusion from me, and left me on Monday morning to face a world from which all heart, charity, kindness and worth had vanished. How she does this, in 10 minutes, between 12 and 1, in the best spare bedroom, with the scent of dried rose leaves about, and a little powder falling on the floor, Heaven knows. Perhaps after 37 undergraduates, mostly the sons of Marquises, one's physical life is reduced, and one receives impressions merely from her drawl and crawl and smell which might be harmless in the stir of normal sunlight. Only is the sunlight ever normal at Garsington? No, I think even the sky is done up in pale yellow silk, and certainly the cabbages are scented. But this is all great rubbish. We've had a desperate afternoon printing, and I'm more in need of the love of my friends than you are. All the 14pt quads have been dissed into the 12 pt boxes! Proof taking has been made impossible; and Eliot's poem delayed a whole week.[7] I'm sure you'll see that this is much more worth crying over than the pox and the fever and the measles all in one. Do you have horrid old gamps who come and cheer you up? by which I mean tell you stories about their past grandeur, and how they have come down in the world or they wouldn't be nursing the likes of you – by which they mean that you haven't got silk chemises. I could write you a whole page about their talk, but refrain.

Here is a quotation from a letter I've just had from Roger, in Salamanca. 'I was really rather surprised to see Saxon Turner[8] approach the table at Segovia where I was seated with one Trend, a Cambridge musician; he approached the table in perfect style with just a little guttural noise, a sort of burble which expressed everything that the moment demanded and sat down and we went about very happily for some days. He became quite talkative. And really what a nice creature he is'. So our poor old Saxon is moving among the living. He disappeared in such gloom, owing to your loss, that I've since thought of him as a kind of sea gull wailing forlornly round the coast on windy nights. You won't be lacking in letters from him. And they will tell you every detail. London is spasmodically gay, that is to say I dine out in humble places and went to the opera one night, and one night to the Italian puppets, and one night to see Nessa, and another to dine with Maynard, and Leonard is frightfully busy. We meet on the stairs oftener than anywhere, and I'm not sure that the glories of the Nation are quite worth so much energy.[9]

Mrs Joad is doing very well – much better, to be honest, than dear old Ralph, but then she is a daily worker, enthusiastic, sanguine, and much impressed by small mercies.[10] If only she didn't scent herself, rather cheaply, I should have nothing to say against her. She is a character so entirely unlike my own that I can't help gaping in astonishment, as we sit at lunch. Fancy playing tennis in Battersea Park! Fancy having a mother who lives at Harpenden! Fancy eating up all the fat, because it's good manners! Carrington insisted on meeting her – I don't think they received good impressions of each other.

(I must omit a passage which contains scurrilous, and probably untrue, reflections on a person now alive.)

Duncan was very severely treated by Simon Bussy in the Nation.[11] Nevertheless he has sold almost every picture, I hear: and they say this will revive poor Roger's miseries about his own failure; but Roger, of course, is far the nicest human being of any of us, and will as usual be incomparably more generous than one could suspect Christ to be, should Christ return, and take to painting in the style of Cézanne at the age of 56. Clive, who has nothing Christlike about him, has had to give up eating tea, because, when Lady Lewis gave a party the other night and Rosenthal played Chopin, a waistcoat button burst and flew across the room with such impetuosity that the slow movement was entirely spoilt.[12] The humiliation, which would have killed you or me – the room was crowded with the élite of London – only brushed him slightly – he won't eat bread and butter any more: but his spirits are superb, and he says that life grows steadily more and more enchanting, the fatter one gets. Mr Bernard Shaw almost agreed to review his book for the Nation;[13] and said so on a postcard, but Clive is very touchy about postcards from Bernard Shaw and has never forgiven Carrington, nor ever will.[14]

(With deep regret I omit a particularly entertaining paragraph which contains statements that may well be true but are certainly libellous.)

I hope you realise that though I am chattering like a pink and yellow cockatoo (do you remember Mrs Brereton's poem, Pink and yellow, pink and yellow?)[15] I'm a chastened raven underneath: I mean I am very much concerned at your miseries, which besides being in themselves odious, show a mean malignity on the part of Providence which makes me, for one, a Christian and a believer. If there were not a God, of course you would have gone to Spain with Saxon: as it is, there you are in bed at Maidstone. Our only alleviation of HIS afflictions is to send you our latest, Talks with Tolstoi – a very amazing book, even when it has passed through the furnace, which I suppose it must do, before reaching you.[16]

Leonard is still trying to take proofs in the basement. I have cheered myself up by writing to you, so please don't say that I've plunged you into despair, as another invalid did the other day, when I cheered myself up by writing to her.[17]

Please get well, and come and see me. Barbara Chickybidiensis is one of those singular blooms which one never sees elsewhere, a rare and remarkable specimen.[18] I wish I could write an article for Outdoor Life about you, and get £50. £25 should then be yours.

Love to Nick.[19]

Let me know how you are.

Yr. V. W.[20]

That Virginia should have written such a letter to one who, as I have said, would not claim to have been of her nearest and dearest, will give some idea of her thoughtful and affectionate nature: the letter itself gives a taste of her gaiety, spirits and power of invention.

But of course it was in conversation that her gaiety poured out most abundantly. Her talk, as my friend Raymond Mortimer would say, was 'dazzling'. It was unlike any other I have heard, though at moments that of Jean Cocteau, at his best, has reminded me of it. To describe conversation is notoriously impossible, and to report it verbatim is not easy. I know it is supposed to be the secret of Boswell's success, but I have sometimes wondered whether Johnson did say exactly what Boswell makes him say. I, at any rate, cannot report conversations word for word: and when I have told the reader that the quality of Virginia's came in part from the apparent whimsicality and from the unexpectedness of her notions and comments, partly from a happy choice of words and constructions, hardly at all from the manner of delivery, but chiefly from sheer magic, I believe I shall not have brought him much nearer the heart of the mystery. The melancholy fact is that till her familiar correspondence has been published, even a vague idea of the fun and spirit of Virginia's talk can hardly be gained by those who did not know her. As the correspondence – or the best part of it – cannot be published, admirers must try to catch a taste of the delicious treat that was her company from passages such as this:

To show how very little control of our possessions we have – what an accidental affair this living is after all our civilisation – let me just count over a few of the things lost in our lifetime, beginning, for that seems always the most mysterious of losses – what cat would gnaw, what rat would nibble – three pale blue canisters of book-binding tools? Then there were the bird cages, the iron hoops, the steel skates, the Queen Anne coal-scuttle, the bagatelle board, the hand organ – all gone, and jewels too. Opals and emeralds, they lie about the roots of turnips. What a scraping paring affair it is to be sure! The wonder is that I've any clothes on my back, that I sit surrounded by solid furniture at this moment. Why, if one wants to compare life to anything, one must liken it to being blown through the Tube at fifty miles an hour – landing at the other end without a single hairpin in one's hair! Shot out at the feet of God entirely naked! Tumbling head over heels in the asphodel meadows like brown paper parcels pitched down a shoot in the post office!

This fragment from that enchanting soliloquy, 'The Mark on the Wall', may perhaps give a hint of what it was like when Virginia indulged in a flight of fancy, as she often did. Of her full length books I think *Orlando* gives the best idea of her with her elbows on the tea-table letting herself go. I am not sure that it is not my favourite of all her works, though of course I do not consider it the best. That, no doubt, is *The Waves*. Indeed, if I were writing as a critic, instead of what they call a 'fan', I should be inclined to say that *The Waves* and perhaps *To the Lighthouse* were the only perfect masterpieces she ever produced. To me *The Waves* seems perfect; whereas I perceive that a stern critic could pick a hole or two in most of the others, and more than two in *Orlando*. Only, if he find fault with *Orlando*, he must find fault with *Tristram Shandy* too; and it seems a pity, should one have the luck to possess a sense of beauty and a sense of humour, to accept grudgingly either of these exquisite satisfactions.

Just now I pictured Virginia with her arms on the tea-table. The image came to mind naturally enough. Often I think of her in the dark dining-room at Rodmell or at the round painted table of Charleston, childishly revelling in cakes and honey, enjoying them as she enjoyed the accompanying gossip and nonsense, herself the life and inspiration of the party. The 'tea-table' I said, and so saying unintentionally gave myself an opportunity of putting a stop to one of the most preposterous lies that ever came into circulation. A year or so before the war I found myself in Paris sitting at dinner next an attractive young French woman who turned out to be a passionate admirer of the novels of my sister-in-law. Naturally she questioned me, and naturally I supplied information of the banal kind one does supply on such occasions. Amongst other things I told her that the artist was handicapped by the constant menace of a nervous disorder which, when it attacked her, made any sort of intellectual effort impossible and reduced her to a state of agitated misery. 'Ah yes', said my pretty neighbour, 'Ah yes', and said it with a sorrowful, meaning look which was not meant to escape me. Quite at a loss, I exclaimed, 'What on earth are you driving at?' 'Well', she said, 'Well, every-body knows – whisky'.[21]

As my old nurse would have said, you could have knocked me down with a feather. As soon as I had recovered my balance I explained that normally Virginia never touched alcohol of any sort, for she did not much like it. Indeed it was a standing joke – every set of intimate friends has its standing jokes – that 'Clive always makes me drunk', by which she meant that when she dined with me I would, if I could, cajole her into drinking a glass of wine or half a glass at any rate. The fact that this grotesque fab-rication appears to have been accepted as true by people who certainly wished Virginia no ill, should be, I suppose, a warning to biographers. I have a fondness for gossip and am perhaps too willing to give mongers the benefit of a doubt. But this bit positively shocks me, not because I object to people getting drunk, but be-cause the notion of Virginia as a dipsomaniac is absurd beyond the limits of absurdity. So I trust that anyone who does me the honour of reading this paragraph, and happens to hear the lie repeated, will do truth the honour of contradicting it flatly.

In my attempts to sketch the characters of other old friends I have adopted the classic method of recalling particular sayings and doings which seemed notably characteristic and pinning them down; but with Virginia that method will not do. Everything she said or did, the way she propounded a theory or uttered an ex-clamation, the way she walked or dressed or did her hair (not very securely), the way she cut a cake (not very neatly), or laughed or sneezed, was peculiar and characteristic. Admirers in search of a memorable image will find my account inadequate, and ad-mirers will be right. As I have sadly admitted more than once, until all the letters and diaries have been published they cannot hope to possess anything like a portrait of the artist: all they can do is to seek her in her books, and these, though of course ex-pressive, do not reveal the whole nor perhaps the most fascinat-ing part. Still, when they have enjoyed her art for its own sake, some are sure to begin wondering just how much of the artist it really does reveal. I will help them in their quest if I can. And now it seems to me possible that by extracting certain passages from that essay – written with Virginia just round the corner and in the knowledge that it would be read and criticised by her – by extracting passages, or elaborating them, I may put the curious on a profitable track.

I then said that what made Virginia Woolf's books read queerly was that they had at once the air of high fantasticality and blazing realism. This, I think, is true, and the explanation may be that, though she is externalising a vision and not making a map of life, the vision is anything but visionary in the vulgar sense of the word. Her world is not a dream world; she sees, and sees acutely, what the reviewer in a hurry calls 'the real world' – the world of Miss Austen and George Eliot, of *Madame Bovary* and *War and Peace*. It is a perfectly comprehensive world in which no one has the least difficulty in believing: only she sees it in her own way. She sees life more purely than most of us see it; and that may mean that sometimes she sees it less passionately. Sometimes she seems to be watching through a cool sheet of glass two lovers (say) on a bench in the park: she will know well enough what they are saying and know (not feel) what they are feeling; she will miss not one subtle, betraying gesture; she will be aware of the romance, but she will not share the romantic emotions. In the strictest sense of the word she is a seer. More often than not her creative impulses spring from her sense of a scene. And this pure, this almost painterlike, vision sets her far apart from the common or garden realists, her contemporaries.

Of course literary art cannot be much like painting; for it is out of words that writers must create the forms that are to clothe their visions, and words carry a significance altogether different from the significance of lines and colours. Virginia, as a matter of fact, had a genuine and highly personal liking for pictures.[22] But her sense of visual values revealed itself most clearly, and characteristically, in a feeling for textures and the relations of textures. She would pick up a feather in the fields and set it in an appropriate wine-glass against a piece of stuff carelessly pinned to the wall, with the taste and 'rightness' of a Klee, if not a Picasso. But that, though I hope it may be of interest to some of her admirers, is beside my immediate point. What I am trying to say is that her vision, and superficially her style, may remind anyone, as it reminded the French critic, M. Abel Chevalley, of the French Impressionists.[23] Her vision may remind us of their passion for the beauty of life, loved for its own sake, of their abhorrence of sentimentality, and of their reputed inhumanity; while technically her style may remind incorrigible seekers after analogy of little touches and divisions of tone. We are familiar with the way in which Renoir and Monet proclaim their sense of a garden blazing in her sun. It is something that comes to them in colours and shapes, and in shapes and colours must be rendered. Now see how an artist in words deals with a like experience.

> How hot it was! So hot that even the thrush chose to hop, like a mechanical bird, in the shadow of the flowers, with long pauses between one movement and the next; instead of rambling vaguely the white butterflies danced one above another, making with their white shifting flakes the outline of a shattered marble column above the tallest flowers; the glass roofs of the palm house shone as if a whole market full of shiny green umbrellas had opened in the sun; and in the drone of the aeroplane the voice of the summer sky murmured its fierce soul. Yellow and black, pink and snow white, shapes of all these colours, men, women and children, were spotted for a second upon the horizon, and then, seeing the breadth of yellow that lay upon the grass, they wavered and sought shade beneath the trees, dissolving like drops of water in the yellow and green atmosphere, staining it faintly with red and blue. It seemed as if all gross and heavy bodies had sunk down in the heat motionless and lay huddled upon the ground, but their voices went wavering from them as if they were flames lolling from the thick waxen bodies of candles. Voices, yes, voices, wordless voices, breaking the silence suddenly with such depth of contentment, such passion of desire, or, in the voices of children, such freshness of surprise; breaking the silence? But there was no silence; all the time the motor omnibuses were turning their wheels and changing their gear; like a vast nest of Chinese boxes all of wrought steel turning ceaselessly one within another the city murmured; on the top of which the voices cried aloud and the petals of myriads of flowers flashed their colours into the air.[24]

No one, I suppose, will deny the beauty of that. No one ever has denied that Virginia Woolf chooses and uses words beautifully. But her style is sometimes accused, injuriously, of being 'cultivated' and 'intellectual' – obviously such criticism would be inapplicable here – especially by people who themselves are not particularly well off for either culture or intellect. Cultivated it is, in the sense that it reveals a finely educated mind on terms of easy acquaintance with the finest minds of other ages; and perhaps it is cultivated also in the sense that to enjoy it a reader must himself be pretty well educated. No doubt it makes unobtrusive reference to and recalls associations with things of which the unlettered dream not. Intellectual? Yes, it is intellectual in that it makes demands on the reader's understanding. However, it is not difficult in the way that the style of philosophers and philosophic writers must be difficult, since it is for visions and states of mind and not for logical processes and abstract reasoning that this author finds verbal equivalents. She has no call to chop logic so her prose can be musical and coloured; also as she has no taste for violence it can be cool. Though colder far, the lyrical passages in her novels are nearer to the last act of *Figaro*, to that music which gives an etherial sense of a summer night's romance, than to the second act of *Tristan* which gives.... Well, the over-sexed will appreciate the art of Virginia Woolf hardly; the fundamentally stupid never.

Yet it cannot be denied that reasonable people have complained – 'Virginia Woolf's novels make stiff reading'. Generally, I think, any trouble they may have in following the movements of her mind is caused not by eccentricity of expression but by the complexity of what is being expressed. For just as there are subtleties of thought which a philosopher cannot, with the best will in the world, make as plain as a police-court statement, so there are subtleties of feeling which an artist cannot express as simply as Tennyson defined his attitude to Lady Clara Vere de Vere.[25] Those who in moments of vexation call her writing unintelligible are, I suspect, unless merely thick-witted, making the mistake that was made by the more enlightened opponents of Impressionism. They are seeking noon at twilight. They are puzzled by a technique which juxtaposes active tones, and omits transitions which have no other function than to provide what modern painters and Virginia Woolf and perhaps the majority of serious contemporary writers hold to be unnecessary bridges. For my part, I shall not deny that I am a little old for jumping, or that in literature I love a bridge, be it merely a plank. My infirmities, however, are unimportant. The important thing is that Virginia Woolf's words and phrases are chosen deliberately, with exquisite and absolute precision, to match her meaning, and that they form a whole which perfectly envelops her vision.

I have tried, by recalling memories and touching on her art, to give what I confessed at the outset would be no more than an adumbration of Virginia Woolf. It now seems to me, re-reading what I have written, that I have failed – and this is perhaps my worst omission – to convey a sense of her magic – for Virginia was a magician in life as well as in art. Can I mend matters, I wonder, by calling to mind at this eleventh hour something that happened many years ago when, after one of her recurrent collapses, she was sent by her doctor to a convalescent home kept by an amiable and commonplace woman called, shall we say, Miss Smith? Although Virginia was ill and intellectually and emotionally below normal her magic within a day or two had done its work; Miss Smith was transformed. Nothing like this had happened to her before; suddenly life, which she had found drab and dreary, had become thrilling and precious. Every moment counted; for everything seemed exciting or amusing. Positively the poor woman started, on the sly, to struggle with the poets; but soon discovered that she had no need for books, her own life, coloured by the presence and idle talk of her patient, having grown poetical. For the first, and I dare say last, time she was living intensely. As she tried to explain to me one afternoon when Virginia, whom I was visiting, was taking a rest, for the first time in her life she felt of consequence to herself; she was aware of her own existence, she said, and all the trivial things that made up that existence had significance too. The magician had cast her spell, and Miss Smith, like any poet, was seeing the world in a grain of sand. Whether the spell endured after the magician had departed I do not know; I should think it unlikely. But during a month or six weeks 'the world' for Miss Smith was 'so full of a number of things' that she, the matron of a nursing home, 'was as happy as' a queen: and I dare say a good deal happier.

This transformation seemed miraculous because the transformed was what is called 'a very ordinary woman'. But the effect of Virginia on her closest friends was not different in kind. I remember spending some dark, uneasy, winter days during the first war in the depth of the country with Lytton Strachey. After lunch, as we watched the rain pour down and premature darkness roll up, he said, in his searching, personal way, 'Loves apart, whom would you most like to see coming up the drive?' I hesitated a moment, and he supplied the answer: 'Virginia of course'. Be sure her magic would have worked on him as it had worked on Miss Smith.

NOTES

Arthur Clive Heward Bell (1881–1964), art critic and writer on literature, married Virginia Woolf's sister Vanessa in 1907.

1. 'Virginia Woolf', *Dial*, 77 (December 1924) 451–65. No such article in *Vanity Fair* is listed in Donald A. Laing's *Clive Bell: An Annotated Bibliography of the Published Writings* (London: Garland, 1983). The typescript is at Trinity College, Cambridge.
2. Pablo Picasso (1881–1973), Spanish painter.
3. 'Preface', *A Writer's Diary, being Extracts from the Diary of Virginia Woolf* (London: Hogarth, 1953) pp. vii–viii.
4. Apparently, Lady Ottoline Morrell.
5. Mary Josefa ('Molly') MacCarthy, née Warre-Cornish (1882–1953), Desmond MacCarthy's wife.
6. Barbara Bagenal, née Hiles (1891–1984), artist.
7. *The Waste Land*, first printed in Eliot's *The Criterion* (1922).
8. Saxon Sydney-Turner (1880–1962), an Apostle and friend of Thoby Stephen at Cambridge, career civil servant in the Treasury.
9. Leonard Woolf was at that time literary editor of *The Nation* (Bell's note).
10. Mrs Joad was working for the Hogarth Press, where she succeeded Ralph Partridge and Barbara Bagenal herself (Bell's note.)
11. See *Nation*, 9 June 1923.
12. I don't think it happened quite like that. For Rosenthal read Rubinstein, probably (Bell's note). [Bell's conjecture appears to be incorrect: Moriz Rosenthal (1862–1946), Ukranian pianist, like Artur Rubinstein, gave London concerts.]
13. Strange, if true; the only thing I published about that time was a little essay 'On British Freedom', it seems unlikely that Bernard Shaw would have heard of it (Bell's note).
14. Carrington had sent me a card, purporting to come from Bernard Shaw and complaining of something I had said about him in print. I was taken in. Carrington and Logan Pearsall Smith were the hoaxers in chief of the age. Personally, I never cared for practical jokes and hoaxes; but when I described them as 'fools' wit' Pearsall Smith took it in bad part. May I add that Carrington and I remained fast friends to the day of her death? (Bell's note).
15. Governess of the Bell children at Charleston in 1917.
16. No: it would have to pass through the furnace – if it passed through the furnace at all – after and not before reaching the invalid (Bell's note).
17. T. S. Eliot's first wife, Vivien.
18. Walking in the garden at Rodmell, Virginia had noticed a flower which struck her as not quite a common nasturtium. She enquired the name. Out came Barbara with 'Tropaeolum Canariensis'. So grand a name, delivered with such authority, by so small a creature, took Virginia's fancy, and she christened her flower-like little friend 'Barbara Chickybidiensis' (Bell's note).

19. Nicholas Beauchamp Bagenal (1891–1974).

20. *Letters*, III, 50–2. Bell's second omission, is, in part, retained.

21. As I have admitted that I cannot report a conversation verbatim, let me further admit that the only words faithfully reproduced here are 'Ah' and 'Whisky': we were talking French (Bell's note).

22. Herself, she occasionally made drawings, which are said to show considerable talent. They accompanied letters which I have not seen (Bell's note).

23. Abel Chevalley (1868–1933), French critic of English literature.

24. 'Kew Gardens'.

25. See Alfred Lord Tennyson's poem 'Lady Clare Vere de Vere' (1842).

Part V
At the Hogarth Press

Tea with a Publisher*

JOHN HOUSEMAN

It was to her [Flora Mayor, the sister of Houseman's Clifton house-master], rather than to my Mayfair friends, that I brought the manuscript of *The Plains* and, on the following Sunday, under the trees of Richmond Park, received her approval.[1] She added (and she hoped I would not mind) that she had sent it on to her own publishers, Leonard and Virginia Woolf at the Hogarth Press. I was appalled.

In the successive emotional stages I had gone through with the book I had only remotely considered the possibility of publication. This sudden, irrevocable exposure of my work to the publishers of Katherine Mansfield, T. S. Eliot, E. M. Forster, Sigmund Freud and Virginia Woolf herself shocked and terrified me. Within ten days a note arrived from Leonard Woolf saying that he and his wife had both read my book and would like to talk to me about it. He understood I worked in the City: how would Saturday tea suit me? I replied that Saturday tea would suit me very well, gave my blue suit to be pressed and carefully combed my hair for my visit to Tavistock Square.

I was received by a dark, slender, soft-spoken man who led me upstairs to a front room, where a lady whom I recognised as Virginia Woolf was seated at the tea table with a schoolboy of twelve or thirteen – a nephew, I gathered.[2] During tea, I became aware of the incessant trembling of Leonard Woolf's hands and of the faint rattle of his cup and saucer, but it was on Mrs Woolf that my attention was fixed. I had read *Jacob's Room*, 'Kew Gardens' and *The Voyage Out* and I had seen her from afar, at night, tall, rustling and brilliant, at Bloomsbury soirées. I had heard of her wit and malice, of her shyness and melancholy. Here at home, behind her teapot, in the afternoon light, she was less formidable,

---

* From *Unfinished Business: A Memoir* (London: Chatto & Windus, 1986; New York: Applause Theatre Books, 1990) pp. 22–4.

with her hooded eyes and noble features, beautiful in a prematurely faded way, talkative, humorous and domestic.

Like film fogged by the brightness of the sun, my memory of that enchanted tea party is blurred and incomplete. I recall the nephew asking some question about H. G. Wells, which Virginia Woolf, smiling, passed on to me and to which I replied, flustered and unprepared, that in my opinion, Mr Wells would be remembered for his prophetic and pseudo-scientific works. Mrs Woolf disagreed. She maintained that Wells's early novels such as *Mr Polly*, *Kipps* and *Tono-Bungay* were works of originality and merit and the rest journalism of no interest whatsoever. Mr Woolf shared her opinion, though less emphatically. After that the conversation became personal: I was asked questions about myself to which, in my desire to shed a more interesting light upon my writing, I gave answers that were only partially true. It was not until tea was over and the nephew had gone back to his homework that my book was mentioned. After nearly fifty years I can still feel myself in that small book-lined room, sitting breathless with delight, hardly hearing the quiet words of praise, spoken first by Mrs Woolf and then by her consort – conscious only of the incredible and overwhelming fact that they liked my book and actually wanted to publish it!

Like most ecstasies it was short-lived. At my second meeting with the Woolfs, Leonard did most of the talking. He confirmed their liking for the work and repeated that he and Virginia would like to publish it at the Hogarth Press. However, as a small house of very limited resources, they were in no position to assume the financial risk that a commercial publisher would normally take with the first work of an author of promise. The Woolfs offered to assume one third of the cost of publication if I could supply the rest.

It must have been my sudden look of dismay that caused Mrs Woolf to break in and explain that all her own books had been published in this way, including *Mrs Dalloway*, which was about to appear. On the other hand, she could understand my reluctance at having to raise money for the publication of my first work; they offered to pass the manuscript on, with their recommendation, to Heinemann's, of which their close friend Desmond MacCarthy was chief editor.

NOTES

John Houseman (1902–88), theatrical and film producer, director and actor. Bucharest-born, Houseman became a naturalised Briton who made his career in the US and was closely associated with Orson Welles in the 1930s. Director of the Juilliard School's drama division (1968–76), Houseman in his later years achieved widespread fame in the television series *The Paper Chase*.

1. Flora Macdonald Mayor (1872–1932), novelist and short-story writer. The Hogarth Press had published her *The Rector's Daughter* in 1924. *The Plains* was a collection of Houseman's stories.
2. That is, Quentin Bell.

Memories of the Hogarth Press*

ELIZABETH HEPWORTH

The Woolfs' country house was at Rodmell, near Charleston. I had several times visited there, and there I was, briefly, offered sanctuary at the time of the 'phoney' war in 1939. A year later, when war broke out in earnest, I was evacuated with others of the Hogarth Press to the Garden City Press at Letchworth, Herts, who were our printers.

At the Hogarth Press, before the war, I was the traveller. We published a small, select list twice a year, so Spring and Autumn I went round the country, England and Wales and also Scotland, collecting orders. The rest of the year I travelled the London bookshops for 'repeats', and in between I worked in the office. I was in charge of the stock, and if anything went astray, despite the fact that I was more often than not 'on the road', I was supposed to bear the blame!

The set-up of the Hogarth Press, in the basement of a house in Tavistock Square, was curious. The Woolfs occupied the main house. A large room at the back of the basement called the Studio was where Virginia wrote her books, and she was not to be disturbed on any account. This studio also housed the book stock.

* *Charleston Newsletter*, no. 17 (December 1986) pp. 9–10.

I was supposed to select and remove each morning, before Virginia came down on the stroke of nine, what I thought would be needed to supply the booksellers' bag-men who would be calling throughout the day. In those times if one ordered a book from a bookshop in the morning one would expect to receive it in the afternoon.

At publishing time it was all hands on deck. Virginia Woolf herself would come down to help with the packing. One of my clearest memories of her is back view, her tall figure bent over the packing-shelf, tying up parcels.

The Woolfs were methodical and punctual to a fault. Leonard Woolf would emerge precisely at a quarter to nine each morning to take the current spaniel dog – in my day it was Sally – into the Square garden, and, as I was myself late, more often than not, I would take advantage of this, as I saw him go, to nip into the office and be where I should be before they got back.

I had been running a bookshop at Dorking, in Surrey, which, in the depression years 1929 and 1930, was doing badly and having to close down. Through one of my customers I had an introduction to Leonard Woolf at a time when his manageress at the Hogarth Press had just died, and the post of 'traveller', or representative, being held by a friend of hers whom Leonard happened not to like, he was looking for replacements for both positions.

I was interviewed for the post of manager. Leonard asked me what I knew about typography: my guardian angel prompted me to tell the truth and I admitted I did not know anything about it! He then switched to the position of 'traveller', and I said that, since I knew the trade from the bookseller's point of view, I thought I might be quite good at that. Leonard then asked me if I could drive a car. I said No, but I'll learn – so I got the job.

Five shillings on the counter of the nearest post office bought me a driving licence. I had a couple of driving lessons; and then I hired a Baby Austin and spent a weekend driving about the quiet country roads around Dorking. It seemed to me a cinch!

Well, Leonard's car was an enormous Lanchester: my feet could hardly reach the controls. He took me to drive a bit in the streets of Bloomsbury near Tavistock Square, where the premises of the Hogarth Press at that time were; and all went well.

So I came to my first day out on the road alone. A day I shall never forget! I stalled the engine in the Euston Road. A bus driver got out of his cab and manoeuvred me on to the side of the road

– since I was holding up all the traffic – where I could calm down and come to my senses. I set off again, but, alas, ran into the back of a van at Notting Hill Gate and buckled the front mudguard. After that all went well and I proceeded down to the coast and got through my day's work without further mishap, except that I had the most flaming headache I have ever had in my life. And I thought that, when I got back, Leonard, who was known to have a fierce temper, would make mincemeat of me.

Nothing of the sort: he was kindness itself. He could see of course that I was very much upset. All he said was 'Oh, that can easily be put right. Don't worry about that'.

During the ten years that I spent with the Hogarth Press I frequently drove Leonard's car. I never had any more trouble with it.

A Boy at the Hogarth Press*

RICHARD KENNEDY

A SOCIAL EVENING WITH THE WOOLFS

I went to supper with the Woolfs. We had strawberries and cream. Mrs W was in a very happy mood. She said she had been to a nightclub the night before and how marvellous it was inventing new foxtrot steps. I thought LW's back looked a bit disapproving as he was dishing out the strawberries. The other guest was George Rylands, a very good-looking young man who had worked for the Woolfs before going to university.[1] We were publishing a book by him called Words and Poetry and McKnight Kauffer had done a design for the cover.[2] George Rylands egged Mrs W on to talk about how much she enjoyed kicking up her heels. I couldn't help feeling a little shocked.

Some people came in with huge bundles of flowers to give her. They had been commissioned to write an article about dirt-track racing. As they were very hard up, they were very anxious to

---

* From A Boy at the Hogarth Press (London: Whittington Press, 1972) pp. 18, 22, 31, 34, 36, 39.

get the job, but the editor had turned down their manuscripts. Mrs W had come to their rescue and written a description of the sport, in which she had compared the roaring machines and the arc lights to a medieval tournament.

Some more people came in after supper. Mrs Woolf started rolling her shag cigarettes. She gave one to an American lady who nearly choked to death.

She started talking about the Hogarth Press in a way that I thought didn't please LW very much, saying it was like keeping a grocer's shop. I think she is rather cruel in spite of the kind rather dreamy way she looks at you. She described Mrs Cartwright as having the step of an elephant and the ferocity of a tiger, which gives a very false impression as Ma Cartwright has no ferocity at all, although she does charge about everywhere. She also described her sliding down the area steps on her bottom, during the frost.

I consider it bad form to laugh at your employees.

JUNE 30, 1928. A LITERARY SWAIN. MRS W AT WORK

Desmond MacCarthy came into the Press and asked to see Mrs W. But she had given strict instructions she was not to be disturbed so he had to content himself with writing her a note. He took about half an hour to do this, leaning on the high school-master's desk which we use as a counter. It would take him a long time to write his articles in the *Sunday Times* at this rate.

In the door that leads into our office from the back there is a square window through which Mrs W can look to see if the coast is clear to enter the office.

When we have exhausted the parcels of fifty copies of each book which are kept in the office, Miss Belcher and I have to enter her studio and manhandle and open one of the very large bales of 500 that are stored there. Sitting in her little space by the gas fire, she reminds me of the Bruce Bairnsfather veterans of the War, surrounded by sandbags.[3] She looks at us over the top of her steel-rimmed spectacles, her grey hair hanging over her forehead and a shag cigarette hanging from her lips. She wears a hatchet-blue overall and sits hunched in a wicker armchair with her pad on her knees and a small typewriter beside her.

SEPTEMBER 5. MRS WOOLF COMPOSES

The Woolfs have returned from Rodmell. Mrs W came into the printing room to set up type. We are printing a new volume of poems by a man called Herbert Palmer.[4] She was in a very gay mood and said she had been on the loose in London. I somehow felt a bit disapproving, perhaps because I am guilty about my own wanderings when I should be at the Press. She reads the most extraordinary books, such as *The Sexual Life of Savages*.[5] She left later with LW and called out to Ma Cartwright for an address. When she was told it was 25, Laburnum Grove, she retailed it to LW as 'The Laurels, Winchester Avenue' and had to be corrected by Ma Cartwright. LW gave a cry of anguish. He is the magician who keeps us all going by his strength of will – like the one in the *Tales of Hoffmann* – and Mrs W is a beautiful magical doll, very precious, but sometimes rather uncontrollable.[6] Perhaps, like the doll, she hasn't got a soul. But when she feels inclined, she can create fantasy and we all fall over ourselves, or are disapproving.

SEPTEMBER 10. A BLOOMSBURY EVENING

The day ended very well, as LW invited me round for the evening to meet the American publisher, Mr Harcourt, who has bought C. H. B. Kitchin's book *Death of My Aunt*, and wants to use my cover design on the American edition.[7]

I sat next to Mrs W who rolled her shag cigarettes on a tray in front of her. I think I must be practically the only person who can smoke them. We drank wine and talked about Lawrence. I thought they meant T. E., but actually it was another Lawrence of whom I had never heard.[8] They discussed what he ought to do in order to make some money. Apparently he suffers from TB. Mrs W held the stage and talked about working class writers being under a disadvantage, like women, as writers. Roger Fry thought it was easier to be a painter than a writer if you were working class, as a painter did not have to have an ear for subtle social distinctions as a writer did. Desmond MacCarthy talked about Gissing.[9] Altogether it was a very uplifting evening and the American publisher, Mr Harcourt, treated me as if I were just as important as any of the others!

A WEEKEND AT RODMELL

Arrived in time for tea. The Woolfs were listening to a talk by
Sir Oliver Lodge on the radio.[10] It interested me, but they were
very contemptuous of him and his belief in a spiritual world.
Desmond MacCarthy came in. He had been out for a walk with
Pinker. He talked about dogs, saying how bored they got. Apparently he works very hard, sitting up till two and three in the
morning writing his articles for the *Sunday Times*. He has a son
who is a medical student and a daughter who is very pretty and
who is trying to get on the stage. Not quite the thing for a member of Bloomsbury to do.

LW and I walked in the garden while Mrs W got the supper
ready. He gave me a book on double-entry book-keeping and
another one on publishing by Unwin, which he said was very
sound. He believes that anyone can do anything they really want
to – that I can master accounts. He says accounts are beautiful
and waste is ugly. He showed me his compost heap with pride.

I got up early as LW had asked me if I liked rising early and I
had assured him I did. The house was quite silent. There was
rather a bad smell about, which I assumed came from the cess-
pool. It was a lovely sunny morning and I walked across the
water meadows to a beautiful stream.

When I got back LW was up smoking his pipe and seemed
pleased to see me. He told me that we were going over to see the
Bells at Charleston for the day. So after breakfast I went with
him in his Singer to Lewes to do some shopping. Children pounded
along the village pavement. 'The first day of school', remarked
LW, his features softening. I thought of the winter term and standing behind the scrum on a sticky day, waiting for someone to
make a break for the line.

We all went for a long walk over the Downs and then had a
picnic. Vanessa Bell fell down a bank on her bottom and I guffawed
with laughter, although no one else even smiled. Somewhere in
the distance came the wail of a child. 'Stung!' cried Mrs W pour-
ing coffee out of a thermos flask. After lunch we all straggled
home over the Downs. LW stopped to have a pee in a very casual
sort of way without attempting to have any sort of cover. I could
see this was a part of his super-rational way of living. Clive Bell
boasted that he was unable to make a cup of tea – which aroused
my contempt. He is the member of the Bloomsbury Set I like the

least. Uncle George tells me that Boris Anrep has depicted Clive
Bell and Diana Guinness in his mosaic on the floor of the National
Gallery.[11] I can well believe this after reading Clive Bell's *Civilization*, which describes people doing nothing but enjoy themselves
while others work to support them. He is the opposite to LW.

NOTES

Richard Kennedy (1910–89), attended the Regent Street Polytechnic and
the Royal College of Art, becoming a prolific illustrator of children's
books.

1. George Humphrey Wolferston ('Dadie') Rylands (b. 1902), bursar,
lecturer and Director of Studies at King's College, Cambridge.
2. Edward McKnight Kauffer (d. 1954), American artist and designer.
The Hogarth Press published Rylands's *Words and Poetry* in May 1928.
3. Charles Bruce Bairnsfather (1888–1959), cartoonist. His most famous
cartoon features two men in a shell-hole at the height of a barrage
with the caption '"Well, if you knows of a better 'ole, go to it"' (*By-
stander*, 24 November 1915).
4. Herbert Edward Palmer (1897–1961), poet and critic.
5. Bronislaw Malinowski's *Sex and Repression in Savage Society* (1927).
6. Dr Miracle and the mechanical doll Olympia of Jacques Offenbach's
opera *Les Contes d'Hoffmann* (1881), based on E. T. A. Hoffmann's tales.
7. C. H. B. Kitchin (1895–1967), novelist, especially of detective novels.
Alfred Harcourt (1881–1954), American publisher.
8. Thomas Edward Lawrence, né Shaw ('Lawrence of Arabia') (1888–
1935), military intelligence officer later in the Royal Air Force, autobiographer. The Lawrence in question is D. H. Lawrence.
9. George Gissing (1857–1903), novelist and short-story writer.
10. Oliver Joseph Lodge (1851–1950; knighted 1902), scientist, also
involved in psychic research.
11. Boris von Anrep (1883–1969), Russian mosaicist. Anrep portrayed
Virginia Woolf herself as 'Clio' in his 'Awakening of the Muses' for the
National Gallery.

Working with Virginia Woolf*

JOHN LEHMANN

When that masterpiece, *The Waves*, was about to be published, Virginia Woolf wrote to me: 'I'm rather dismayed to hear we've printed 7,000: for I'm sure 3,000 will feed all appetites; and then the other 4 will sit round me like decaying corpses for ever in the Studio'.[1]

I was working at the time as manager, or rather probationary manager, of the Hogarth Press, and it was my business, with Leonard Woolf, to shepherd all the books through the printers and to see that sufficient copies were ready before publication. As a matter of fact, Virginia Woolf need not have worried. *The Waves* was an immediate success, and far more than 7,000 copies were eventually sold. There were no decaying corpses to sit round her for ever. But what an extraordinary picture that conjures up; what an extraordinary remark for an author to make, one might say, if one did not know that Virginia Woolf was in the unusual, and on the whole agreeable, position of acting as her own publisher.

In those days the Hogarth Press was established in the basement of number 52 Tavistock Square – a house that disappeared in the blitz. The studio was at the back, a large-ish room with a dusty top light, and there Virginia had her work desk. All round the desk, fencing it in with weird and ever-changing architecture, were piles of Hogarth Press books in their brown paper parcels, just as they came from the binders. Virginia had some reason for calling them corpses, for it was only those books for which the urgent demand had ceased that were put into the studio. The newly published books and the best-sellers were outside, in the corridor. If they had gone into the studio, there would have been too many interruptions for even Virginia's patience and powers of concentration. As it was, nearly every day two or three calls had to be made for books that were suddenly needed

---

* *Listener*, 13 January 1955, pp. 60–2.

on the packing table in the front room: I used to slip in as silently as possible, to hunt them out, feeling that I was entering the holiest part of the house, the inmost ark of its presiding deity.

The studio was an epitome and illustration of Virginia Woolf's double life: her life as an author and her life as a publisher of that author – and of many other authors as well. The publishing life encroached without respite on the writing life. It may have been maddening at times: one of the chief reasons why both she and her husband were so anxious to train a young man to follow in their footsteps was to be rid of this encroachment. It may have been aggravating beyond measure to be exposed to the vain bores, the unsnubbable fanatics, who make publishers their targets, their St Sebastians; but there were, I believe, compensations all the same – compensations that were of real importance to Virginia Woolf.

Among the many misconceptions of her that have gained currency since her death, the picture of her as an over-refined *précieuse ridicule*, a person of etiolated sensibility without humour – or only arch or whimsical humour – is the most absurd. Anyone who is deeply acquainted with her work will, I believe, know how absurd a picture it is; let alone anyone who knew her personally. But in her *Writer's Diary* – or rather in those parts of it which Leonard Woolf has seen fit to publish – she has revealed how passionately she cared about her writing, with what unbearably sensitive nerves she reacted to criticism of her work. How wonderful it is to see this professional passion – and also this honesty about what nearly all artists feel but most of them are ashamed to admit. But the diary, as published may nevertheless have created another kind of false impression. The passion, the exposed nerves, were a reality all right; but there was another side to her, a practical side, a side of sharp observation and wit about the outside world, that balanced the inward, imaginative intensity; and it was precisely that side to which her work for the Hogarth Press so effectively gave play.

The business management she left almost entirely to Leonard Woolf and to me; but she took an extremely active part in reading and in deciding on the manuscripts that came in, in planning new series and in persuading authors to write for them. She also liked to help in the office when there was a rush on. She would put herself to work at the packing table with the rest of us, and devote sometimes a whole afternoon to the boring and exhausting business of doing up parcels and labelling them – unrecognised by most of the callers, some of whom would dearly have loved to catch a glimpse of her.

She also enjoyed type-setting. The Hogarth Press had started with a small hand-printing machine, and even when it had become an important publishing firm, the Woolfs faithfully kept up the tradition of printing one or two little books of poems or pamphlets every year themselves. By the time I arrived in 1931 the hand-machine had been exchanged for a larger treadle machine that could sometimes be persuaded to work off the electric current. It was housed in a disused scullery up the passage, and was used mainly for rolling off the firm's writing paper, the invoices, royalty forms, review slips and rejection slips. That work was done by Leonard; but when one of the poetry books was in production, Virginia would generally set the type there by hand; then Leonard would take over and transfer the type to the formes. I think a certain element of pious attachment to the early adventurous days entered into this; but I also think that Virginia Woolf found such humdrum manual labour particularly soothing and restoring after her work on one of the novels. 'What a heaving *The Waves* was, that I still feel the strain!', she wrote in her diary one day.[2] Packing up parcels and setting the type for poems were like a quiet walk along the sea-shore after all the heaving and tossing.

My relations with Virginia began with an ardent youthful hero-worship; but gradually, as I got to know her better through working with her in the Hogarth Press, this turned into a feeling of real affection as well as respect. I found her the most enchanting of friends, full of sympathy and understanding for my own personal problems as well as the problems I was up against in my job. She had the liveliest curiosity about my own life and the lives of my friends in my generation – many of them were known and even related to her. She liked to hear all about what we wanted to do in poetry, in painting, in novel-writing. She would stimulate me to talk, for she had a unique gift for encouraging one to be indiscreet, and would listen with absorption, interspersing pointed and witty comments.

Some of the happiest times I can remember in those years were the luncheons and teas they would invite me up to during the working day: they lived on the top two floors of number 52, in rooms fabulous for me on account of their wall paintings by Duncan Grant and Vanessa Bell – paintings so strangely exposed to the public gaze when a Nazi bomb ripped through the house ten

years later. There we would discuss the publishing plans of the
Press, the manuscripts submitted to us, and all the histories and
personalities involved. She was always bubbling with ideas, longing
to launch new schemes and produce books that no one had thought
of before, that would startle the conventional business minds of
the book world. She found an all too ready response in me, and
we would sometimes have to be quietly checked on the rein by
Leonard Woolf.

One of these schemes that we hatched together was the little
series of Hogarth Letters, that were published as shilling pamphlets with a brightly coloured cover design of a writing hand
by John Banting. E. M. Forster, Francis Birrell, Rebecca West,
Leonard Strong, Raymond Mortimer, Viscount Cecil, and my sister
Rosamond had all contributed, and the series was enjoying some
success.[3] I was very anxious for Virginia to contribute one on
poetry; we had talked so much about poetry together that I thought
it was high time for her to define her views about it. I made this
suggestion at the end of an enthusiastic letter I wrote to her about
The Waves, an advance copy of which I had just read. In answer
she wrote the letter from which I have already quoted at the beginning; a letter as interesting for the light she throws on her
own intentions in *The Waves* as for her characteristic reaction to
my suggestion. She says about *The Waves*:

> I agree that it's very difficult – bristling with horrors, though
> I've never worked so hard as I did here, to smooth them out.
> But it was, I think, a difficult attempt – I wanted to eliminate
> all detail; all fact; and analysis; and myself; and yet not be frigid
> and rhetorical; and not monotonous (which I am) and to keep
> the swiftness of prose and yet strike one or two sparks, and
> not write poetical, but purebred prose, and keep the elements
> of character; and yet that there should be many characters, and
> only one; and also an infinity, a background behind – well, I
> admit I was biting off too much.
>
> But enough, as the poets say. If I live another 50 years I think
> I shall put this method to some use, but as in 50 years I shall
> be under the pond, with the gold fish swimming over me, I
> daresay these vast ambitions are a little foolish, and will ruin
> the press. That reminds me – I think your idea of a Letter most
> brilliant – To a Young Poet? – because I'm seething with im-
> mature and ill considered and wild and annoying ideas about

prose and poetry. So lend me your name – (and let me sketch a character of you by way of frontispiece) – and then I'll pour forth all I can think of about you young, and we old, and novels – how damned they are – and poetry, how dead. But I must take a look into the subject, and you must reply, 'To an old novelist' – I must read Auden, whom I've not read, and Spender (his novel I swear I will tackle tonight).[4] The whole subject is crying out for letters – flocks, volleys of them, from every side. Why not get Spender and Auden and Day Lewis[5] to join in? But you must go to Miss Belsher, and I must go to my luncheon.

This is only a scribble to say how grateful I am for your letter.

In the excitement of the publication of *The Waves* and the first public reactions to it, the idea of a *Letter to a Young Poet* was lost sight of for some weeks. However, Virginia Woolf was turning it over in her mind all the time, and just before she returned to London at the end of summer from her Sussex home, she wrote to me again:

I dont suppose there's anything for me to say about modern poetry, but I daresay I shall plunge, at your bidding. We must talk about it. I dont know what your difficulties are. Why should poetry be dead? etc. etc. But I wont run on, because then I shall spurt out my wild theories, and I've had not a moment to read for days and days. Everybody in the whole world has been here...And now I should be packing. And then we go back. And then there'll be all the books fluttering about us; alas: it's going to be a bad season I'm afraid.

But I want to go into the question of poetry all the same.[6]

This passage shows that she was already beginning to change her mind about poetry being dead; and when the *Letter to a Young Poet* was finally written,[7] she made a spirited attack on the idea that poetry was necessarily dying, or that the obscurity and introversion of much of my contemporaries' work (which she was now reading) proved that it was dying:

...consider the symptoms. They are not the symptoms of death in the least. Death in literature, and I need not tell you how often literature had died in this country or in that, comes gracefully, smoothly, quietly. Lines slip easily down the accustomed grooves. The old designs are copied so glibly that we are half-inclined to think them original, save for that very glibness. But here the very opposite is happening: here in my first quotation the poet breaks his machine because he will clog it with raw fact. In my second, he is unintelligible because of his desperate determination to tell the truth about himself.

Virginia Woolf encouraged me to controversy about the views she had put forward in her *Letter.* As one of the poets whom she had honoured by quoting, I was too pleased to want to dispute her belief that poetry was *not* entering a period of decadence; but I tried to take her up on other points. She had made fun of young writers' fondness for 'dressing up', for pretending that literature was full of heroes and villains, of new movements in melodramatic conflict with old movements. I maintained that there was no harm in it, it was a good stimulant, and had been practised by many admirable English and French poets in the past. She replied that gin and bitters was as good a stimulant; and that the trouble about it was that it became a habit and froze one into ridiculous poses as one grew older. I also claimed that there was no harm in a poet publishing early, because it wiped the slate clean and gave him the kick of a new start; her argument was that on the contrary it engraved the slate in a fatally enduring way.

But our chief point of difference was over 'Mrs Gape', the symbolic charwoman figure she had taken to represent the intractable realistic material we were trying to use in our poetry. I felt that this was the weakest part of a brilliant piece of work: Mrs Gape was nothing but a fantasy of Virginia Woolf's, a fantasy that corresponded to nothing we were trying to assimilate, and her idea of 'beauty' seemed oddly conventional. In her reply to the letter in which I tried to say all this, she admitted she had chosen quotations that were weak for her argument, but she returned – and I think effectively – to the attack by saying that her complaint was that the poet, in tackling his new material, 'didn't dig himself in deep enough'; and she went on:

[He] wakes up in the middle; his imagination goes off the boil; he doesnt reach the unconscious automated state – hence the spasmodic, jerky, self conscious effect of his realistic language. But I may be transferring to him some of the ill effects of my own struggles the other way round – writes poetry in prose.

Tom Eliot I think succeeds; but then he is much more violent; and I think by being violent, limits himself so that he only attacks a minute province of his imagination; whereas you younger and happier spirits should, partly owing to him, have a greater range and be able to devise a less steep and precipitous technique. But this is mere guesswork of course...[8]

I have given this brief history of the *Letter to a Young Poet* because it shows, I think, not only how keenly Virginia Woolf was ready to be interested in the ideals and struggles of a younger generation of writers, but also how much she enjoyed playing her part in all the activities of the Hogarth Press. She wanted the Press to find new writers, to get new projects going all the time. The Hogarth Letters series was one of these projects that particularly appealed to her; and it was all part of the game that she should write one of the Letters herself. If it had not been for that professional feeling, she would never have written the *Letter to a Young Poet* – perhaps never bothered to put down her ideas about the modern poetry of that time at all.

Nevertheless, I suspect that the labour and responsibilities of a publisher's life were felt by her increasingly, as the years went by, to be more of a burden than they were worth. The chief burden fell on Leonard Woolf; but the Press tied them both, and Virginia was unable to get away for sufficiently long spells of creative work. I left the Press and London before I became a fully-fledged manager, but half-a-dozen years later, looking for a new publisher for my already established *New Writing*,[9] I went to see them again and found them more anxious than ever to shift the burden on to younger shoulders. So it was that I returned to the Hogarth Press in the year before the outbreak of war, and became a partner in Virginia Woolf's place. When the agreement came into force, she wrote to me:

I'm full of sanguininity about the future: and thankful to lift the burden onto your back. Nor can I see myself any reason why we should quarrel; or why we should drink the Toast in cold water. What about a good dinner (not English) at Boulestin or some such place? You are hereby invited to be the guest of Virginia Woolf's ghost – the Hogarth ghost: who lives let us hope elsewhere. Lets arrange it. We come back on Sunday: and then there'll be the usual uproar.[10]

It would be wrong to suggest that the new arrangement immediately resulted in Virginia Woolf's retirement. The Press had moved, printing machine and all, to 37 Mecklenburgh Square, and there the same discussions over luncheon and tea, the same absorbing arguments about new projects and new authors went on, for some time, much as before. Gradually, however, Virginia Woolf, absorbed in her biography of Roger Fry, let the distance increase between herself and her old responsibilities; and when Mecklenburgh Square was badly damaged in the first weekend of the blitz, she and Leonard abandoned London and made a permanent headquarters of their Sussex home. I was left in almost complete charge of the Press.

One of my chief pleasures hitherto had been in hearing Virginia describe whatever book she was at work on, the stage it had reached and the difficulties she was encountering. Now, seeing her only on rare occasions, I was cut off from this. It was therefore a complete surprise to me to hear, one day in the spring of 1941, that she had just completed a new novel. I can remember the occasion well: we were all three meeting for luncheon at St Stephen's Tavern near the House of Commons, to discuss the business of the Press. I had sent them Terence Tiller's first book of poems, with a strong recommendation that we should accept it.[11] They had brought it with them, and Virginia immediately told me that she liked it, and thought we ought to publish it. It was the last book she was ever to read and approve for the Press.

I had noticed that she seemed in a state of unusual tension; but when the big news about *Between the Acts* was revealed, I assumed it was only due to her excitement about that. She began to talk with increasing agitation about it, saying that it was no good at all and obviously could not be published. Leonard opposed her, and as I pleaded to be allowed to read it and give my opinion, she agreed to send me the manuscript when she got back to the country. At the same time she complained that she had nothing to do, and asked if I could send her some of the manuscripts that were coming in for *New Writing*. Looking back on that request afterwards, when the tragedy had happened, I realised that her need to have something to occupy and calm her mind was already desperately urgent.

A few days later the typescript of *Between the Acts* reached me, with a letter from her repeating her doubts but asking me to give the casting vote. I plunged into it, at once, and finished it, I remember, just before I had to go on Home Guard night duty. I thought about it all that night. The typing – even the spelling – was more eccentric than I had ever seen in one of her manuscripts: that, and the corrections she had made all over the pages, communicated an extraordinary impression, as if a high voltage electric current had been in her fingers. But I had no doubts at all about the brilliance of the book or the importance of publishing it, and I sent her a telegram to say so next morning. It was too late. Her breakdown had started – she was seriously ill – and both she and Leonard realised that she could not possibly revise the book until she had recovered. 'Please forgive me', she wrote, 'and believe I'm only doing what is best'.[12] In a separate package she returned the manuscripts I had sent her, with lucid and perceptive notes of criticism attached to each. It was her last work for the Hogarth Press – and with me. By the time the package reached me, Virginia Woolf was dead.

NOTES

Rudolph John Frederick Lehmann (1907–87), poet, editor, publisher and literary critic. General manager and a partner in the Hogarth Press (1938–46), he later directed his own publishing house. He founded and edited the highly regarded and influential *New Writing* and the *London Magazine*.

1. Letter of 17 September [1931], *Letters*, IV, 380–1.
2. Entry for 13 January 1932, *Diary*, IV, 62.
3. Leonard Arthur George Strong (1896–1958), writer, journalist and publisher. Rosamond Nina Lehmann (1901–90), novelist.
4. Wystan Hugh Auden (1907–73), poet. Spender had submitted a novel to the Hogarth Press which was rejected and which Woolf suggested he abandon rather than rewrite. For information about Stephen Spender, see p. 187.
5. Cecil Day Lewis (1904–72), poet, translator, Professor of Poetry at Oxford, Poet Laureate 1968–72.
6. Letter of [30 September 1931], *Letters*, IV, 383.
7. *A Letter to a Young Poet* (Hogarth Press, 1932).
8. Letter of 31 July [1932], *Letters*, V, 83.
9. Established by Lehmann in 1935 and issued at about half-yearly intervals until 1940, publishing the 'younger generation' of writers including W. H. Auden, Stephen Spender and Christopher Isherwood.
10. Letter of 22 April [1938], *Letters*, VI, 224. The toast was to celebrate Lehmann's partnership in the Hogarth Press.
11. Terence Rogers Tiller (1916–87), educator, playwright and poet.
12. Letter of [27? March 1941], *Letters*, VI, 486.

Part VI
Pen Portraits

Virginia Stephen*

DUNCAN GRANT

I first knew Virginia Stephen when she and her brother Adrian took No. 29 Fitzroy Square, soon after her sister Vanessa married Clive Bell.[1] It was a house on the south-west corner of the square with a view of the two fine Adams' façades. It was a derelict square. The houses of the great had gradually decayed and were taken as offices, lodgings, nursing homes and small artisans' workshops.

I had taken for a studio two rooms on the second floor of a house on the same side of the square. There was certainly not much gentility left in the district; the only relic of grandeur was a beadle to march round the square and keep order among the children, in a top-hat and a tail-coat piped with red and brass buttons. The Stephens were the only people I remember who had a complete house there; complete with their cook Sophie Farrell, their maid Maud, a front-door bell and a dog, Hans. A close friendship sprang up between Adrian Stephen and myself, and I had only to tap at the window of the ground-floor room to be let in. 'That Mr Grant gets in everywhere', Maud once remarked to Virginia. But irregular as my visits were, in a sense they soon became frequent enough to escape notice.

The house was conveniently divided to suit the inhabitants. On the ground floor was Adrian's study lined with books. Behind was the dining room. The first floor was entirely a drawing room – the room least used in the house. It was a pleasantly proportioned room, with long windows overlooking the square. It had a green carpet, red brocade curtains; a Dutch Portrait of a Lady and Watts' portrait of Sir Leslie Stephen were the only pictures on the walls.[2] In the back part of the room there was an instrument called a Pianola, into which one put rolls of paper punctured by small holes. You bellowed with your feet and Beethoven or Wagner would appear.

* *Horizon*, 18 no. 3 (June 1941) pp. 402–6.

Anyone coming into the room might have thought that Adrian was a Paderewski – the effort on the bellows gave him a swaying movement very like that of a great performer, and his hands were hidden.

I do not remember that Virginia ever performed on this instrument, but it must have played a part in her life, for Adrian on coming home from work would play in the empty room by the hour. Entirely empty it nearly always was and kept spotlessly clean.

It was here that Virginia sometimes saw her less intimate friends and it was here that the dog Hans made mess on the hearthrug when Lady Strachey was paying her first visit, and no mention was made of the fact by either lady.

The more lively rooms were Virginia's own workroom above this, and Adrian's downstairs. Her room was full of books untidily arranged and a high table at which she would write standing. The windows on this floor were double. She was very sensitive to sound, and the noise from the mews and street was severe. The time she gave to her writing was two and a half hours in the morning. She never, I believe, wrote for more than this time, but very regularly.

The study on the ground floor had the air of being much lived in. It was to this room that their friends came on Thursday evenings – a continuation of those evenings which began in Gordon Square before Thoby Stephen died and before Vanessa married. It was there that what has since been called 'Bloomsbury' for good or ill came into being.

About ten o'clock in the evening people used to appear and continue at intervals till twelve o'clock at night, and it was seldom that the last guest left before two or three in the morning. Whisky, buns and cocoa were the diet, and people talked to each other. If someone had lit a pipe he would sometimes hold out the lighted match to Hans the dog, who would snap at it and put it out. Conversation; that was all. Yet many people made a habit of coming, and few who did so will forget those evenings.

Among those who constantly came in early days were Charles Sanger, Theodore Llewelyn Davies, Desmond MacCarthy, Charles Tennyson, Hilton Young (now Lord Kennet), Lytton Strachey.[3]

It was certainly not a 'salon'. Virginia Stephen in those days was not at all the sort of hostess required for such a thing. She appeared very shy and probably was so, and never addressed the company. She would listen to general arguments and occasionally speak, but her conversation was mainly directed to someone next to her. Her brother's Cambridge friends she knew well by this time, but I think there was always something a little aloof and even a little fierce in her manner to most men at the time I am speaking of. To her women friends, especially older women like Miss Pater and Miss Janet Case, who had taught her Greek, she was more open and less reserved.[4] They were alive to her, by remembrance as well as presence, and had already their place in her imagination as belonging to the world she knew and had left – that life with her parents and her half-brothers at Hyde Park Gate. Henceforward she and her brother and sister had tacitly agreed to face life on their own terms.

I do not think that her new existence had 'become alive' to Virginia's imagination in those first years. She gave the impression of being so intensely receptive to any experience new to her, and so intensely interested in facts that she had not come across before, that time was necessary to give it a meaning as a whole. It took the years to complete her vision of it.

It is very difficult for one who is no writer to attempt to describe so subtle a thing as the 'feeling' of long ago. But I must make the attempt to explain why it was that the effect of these young people on a contemporary was so remarkable. To begin with they were not Bohemians. The people I had come across before who had cut themselves off from respectable existence had been mainly painters and Bohemians. If the Stephens defied the conventions of their particular class, it was from being intellectually honest.

They had suffered much, had struggled and finally arrived at an attitude of mind which I think had a great influence on their friends.

If it was an influence Virginia Stephen and her sister were unconscious of the fact.

The impression generally given must have been that these two young women were absorbing the ideas of their new Cambridge friends. And of course this was true up to a point. Saxon Sydney Turner, Clive Bell, Lytton Strachey, Maynard Keynes, were willing to discuss anything and everything with them or before them. It was a gain all round. What the Cambridge of that time needed was a little feminine society. It was a little arid, and if it took almost everything seriously it had mostly left the Arts out of account. It took some things religiously. 'This is my Bible' was said by one, pointing to the *Principia Ethica*, by G. E. Moore.[5] This eminent philosopher was certainly the overwhelming influence on these young men. Conversations on the 'Good' and the value of certain states of mind were a frequent subject of discussion; and these Apostolic young men found to their amazement that they could be shocked by the boldness and scepticism of two young women.

To be intimate with Virginia Stephen in those days was not to be on easy terms. Indeed the greater the intimacy the greater the danger – the danger of sudden outbursts of scathing criticism. I have the impression that no one had much encouragement for anything they produced. Nor was it looked for. Nothing was expected save complete frankness (of criticism) and a mutual respect for the point of view of each. To work for immediate success never entered anyone's head, perhaps partly because it seemed out of the question. Virginia Stephen was working on her first novel, *The Voyage Out*.[6] It took seven years to finish. But I do not remember that this was thought to be an out of the way length of time in which to produce a novel.

The inner fierceness of her attitude to which I have already alluded is worth remembering, and will possibly surprise those who only knew her in later life when it seemed to have entirely disappeared or to have found expression in quite other ways.

It then expressed itself sometimes, as I have said, by an appearance of acute shyness. Upon an unforeseen introduction, for instance, there was an expression of blazing defiance, a few carefully chosen banalities, and a feeling of awkwardness. It came from a sort of variant of Cézanne's *grapin dessous*, which made her literally turn tail from misadventure. As when she saw Mrs Humphry Ward[7] advancing along a narrow passage in the Louvre and hid herself behind a totally inadequate post.

No one so beautiful and so fierce could give offense except to the very stupid. But she was capable of inspiring feelings of respect in the most philistine.

This shyness or fierceness was a necessary self-defence in her war with the world. The world must, she surmised, accept her on her own terms or not at all.

If these notes have any interest it is because they may to some revive the memory, to others suggest the existence, of that seemingly very different Virginia Woolf known to a variety of people in later years.

Marriage and possibly a growing appreciation of her work had the effect of seeming to make her very much more at ease in the world.

NOTES

Duncan James Corrowr Grant (1885–1978), painter. Known especially for his decorative work, Grant was a member of Roger Fry's Omega Workshop. The companion of Vanessa Bell after the failure of her marriage to Clive Bell, he lived with her at Charleston, Sussex.

1. Virginia and Adrian Stephen moved to Fitzroy Square in late March 1906. Vanessa Stephen married Clive Bell on 7 February.
2. G. F. Watts (1817–1904), painter, sculptor and portraitist.
3. Charles Percy Sanger (1871–1930), economist and barrister. Theodore Llewelyn Davies (1871–1905). Charles Bruce Loclar Tennyson (1879–1977; knighted 1945), the poet's grandson and biographer, later in industry. Edward Hilton Young (1879–1960; peerage 1935), barrister, journalist and parliamentarian.
4. Clara Pater tutored Woolf in Latin in 1900. Janet Elizabeth Case (1862–1937), classical scholar devoted to feminist and liberal causes.
5. Influential work, published in 1903, by George Edward Moore (1873–1958), Cambridge philosopher.
6. The novel was possibly inspired as early as 1904. Woolf began an early version entitled *Melymbrosia* in 1907–8, and much altered and renamed, it was accepted in 1913 and published in 1915.
7. Mary Augusta Ward (1851–1920), novelist.

A Life 'rich in experience'*

WILLIAM PLOMER

Once when Virginia Woolf was sitting beside Lady Ottoline on a sofa their two profiles were suddenly to be seen, one in relief against the other, like two profiles on some Renaissance medal – two strange, queenly figures evolved in the leisured and ceremonious days of the nineteenth century. Each, by being herself, won an allegiance to herself in the twentieth. Both faces were aristocratic, but in that chance propinquity Virginia Woolf's appeared much the more fine and delicate. The two women admired one another, with reservations on one side at least; and they were affectionate in manner when together, though one appeared more affectionate than the other. They had a good deal in common. Both had what old-fashioned people used to call *presence* – a kind of stateliness, a kind of simple, unfussy dignity. Lady Ottoline Morrell, not always discriminating about people, recognised the uniqueness of Virginia Woolf. Virginia Woolf spoke admiringly of the independence and force of character which had enabled Lady Ottoline to emerge from the grand but narrow world into which she had been born (and of which she retained the panache) into a more varied world in which ideas and talent counted more than property or background.

Both had an insatiable curiosity about their fellow-creatures, and both a love of gossip and the capacity to be amused or astonished which goes with that virtue. In the exercise of this curiosity the difference of approach was as striking as the difference in their profiles. Lady Ottoline would ask the most personal, direct questions, not in a hectoring way, but without the slightest compunction, and with the manner of a feudal grandee who had a right to be told what she wanted to know. Because most people like talking about themselves to a sympathetic listener she often got what she wanted, but not from me.

* From *The Autobiography of William Plomer* (London: Jonathan Cape, 1975; New York: Taplinger, 1976) pp. 254–9.

Virginia Woolf's approach was less blunt and more ingenious. With a delicious and playful inventiveness she would often improvise an ironical fantasy about the life and habits of the person to whom she was talking, and this was likely to call forth protests, denials, and explanations which helped to make up something like a confession. Lady Ottoline, less tense and less discerning, was an easier mixer: Virginia Woolf sometimes frightened people by aloofness or asperity, for which they had sometimes their own clumsiness to blame. Yet she could show the most graceful restraint. In the course of several hours of the company of an individual who, she afterwards told me, caused her alternating emotions of anger, laughter, and utter boredom, she showed no sign of the first two and only a faint trace of the last – which is the most difficult of the three to hide.

The fact that Virginia Woolf did not make, either in social life or in her books, any concession to vulgarians, or offer any foothold to a banal understanding, or bait any traps for popularity, probably helped to create a legend about herself among the uninformed, the envious, and the ignorant, that she was some sort of precious and fragile being, ineffably superior and aloof, and quite out of touch with 'ordinary' life – whatever that may be. This legend has been completely dispersed. It is now understood that her life was rich in experience of people and places, and that her disposition, as is sometimes the case with those who are highly strung and have an inclination to melancholy, was genial.

Her biographers, so far from having to chronicle the life of an etiolated recluse, may be embarrassed by the quantity and variety of their material. Clearly no adequate biography will be possible until her immense diary has been published in full. From her conversation I recall many interesting glimpses and facets of her earlier life – how, as a young girl, in an agony of shyness, she drove alone at night in a cab with straw on the floor to a ball at one of the great London houses, wearing no jewellery except a modest string of pearls ('but they were *real* pearls'); how she had Greek lessons with Clara, the sister of Walter Pater, in Canning Place, in a setting of blue China, Persian cats, and Morris wallpapers; how she took part in the Dreadnought Hoax, one of the world's great practical jokes and a superb piece of acting, a demonstration that high-ranking hearts of oak at Portsmouth were accompanied by heads of the same material, since they were unable to see through a bogus Negus of Abyssinia and his preposterous 'suite'; how she went bathing with Rupert Brooke, whose profile was not quite lived up to by his legs, those being perceptibly bowed; how she sat up all night in a Balkan hotel reading the *Christian Science Monitor* to cheat the bugs; and how there was a murder under her window in Euboea.

Speaking of writing as a profession, she once remarked to me that one is bound to upset oneself physically if one works for more than two hours a day. She put so much of herself into her work that it must have taken much out of her, and she was in fact a prodigiously hard worker. The volume of her published and unpublished writings, including her letters and diary, is as impressive as the sustained high level of all that has so far been printed. She was as energetic as her father, to whom mountains were no obstacles, nor mountains of fact either.

To be so active, one's nature must be integrated. In each of us there are two beings, one solitary and one social. There are persons who cannot bear to be with others, and turn into hermits or something worse; most cannot bear to be alone, and become common or shallow, or both. In Virginia Woolf the two beings seemed to have an equal life and so to make her into a complete person. She could be detached and see things in perspective; and she could enter into things, into other people's lives, until she became part of them. The two beings can be perceived in her writings, sometimes distinct, sometimes merged. The special genius of her rare and solitary spirit reached its purest expression in *The Waves*, an exquisite, subjective book nearer to poetry and music than to what is generally meant by 'the novel'. The social being in Virginia Woolf, and (in my opinion) the novelist, can be seen most clearly not in her fiction but in *The Common Reader*. Those essays are full of shrewdness and knowledge of the world and of human nature, qualities which, though discernible in her novels, are less important to them than her own sensitivity, as an instrument to the vibrations of the external world.

The old masters of fiction – Shakespeare, Balzac, Tolstoy – are such because, besides all the other gifts, they are imaginative men of the world with an exceptional robustness and gusto. They have also an extreme preoccupation with sociology. This, when it goes more with finesse than with animal spirits, produces novelists like Jane Austen, Flaubert, or Proust, and it was to such writers that Virginia Woolf was in some ways akin. It may be argued that her myth-making faculty was chiefly applied to sensation rather than to characters, and that her passion for sociology was in a sense scientific. Although she enjoyed embroidering facts about people, sometimes in a poetic or a fantastic or a censorious or an ironical way, she was really devoted to the facts themselves. The solitary being was a poet, the social being was a sort of scientist: the former discovered poetic truth, the latter anthropological truth.

During the last ten years of her life Virginia Woolf several times told me how much more she enjoyed reading autobiographies than novels. She once said she thought almost any autobiography more satisfying than a novel. When autobiographical memoirs were written by people she knew and found congenial – Lady Oxford, for instance (and what a sharp profile there!), or the bluff and breezy Dame Ethel Smyth – she not only had the pleasure of getting to know them better, but her appetite for social knowledge and reminiscence was much gratified.[1] A passionate precision in collecting data about society (very strong in Flaubert and Proust) made her delight in anything that helped it.

At those evenings in Tavistock Square she was at her best with persons who, like herself, were not merely articulate but articulate in a new way. She had a gift for making the young and obscure feel that they were of value too. She admired physical as well as intellectual beauty. She could charm away diffidence, and, since she was something of a feminist, could be notably sympathetic with young women, in particular young women from Cambridge. A strong sense of the proper functions of literature and a highly and constantly cultivated taste gave her a proper pride (derived in part no doubt from her literary father and background) in her own gifts, but she was without arrogance, and wore her rare beauty without ostentation.

It is not enough to say that she was a hard-working writer, and that she always read a great deal. She also worked as publisher, and even at times as a printer, with her husband. She examined a great number of typescripts and even of manuscripts for the Hogarth Press, books from which rightly bore the imprint of 'Leonard and Virginia Woolf'. As early as 1930 she and her husband expressed some annoyance at the way the Hogarth Press was developing. They even seemed half vexed by the increasingly profitable sales of Hogarth Press books, and were seriously considering reducing the press to its original and remarkable dimensions – a hand-press in a basement at Richmond, worked by themselves as amateurs. This was before John Lehmann was inducted into the business and began his long and conspicuous career as a publisher and editor. From the time I first saw him he showed an interest in my writings which has continued to this day, and I am only one of innumerable writers whom he has helped.

Virginia Woolf loved London and the country, her relations, and friends; she loved her domestic surroundings; she loved the written word. She liked good talk, good food, and good coffee. I see her in a shady hat and summer sleeves, moving between the fig tree and the zinnias at Rodmell; I see her sitting over a fire and smoking one of her favourite cheroots; I see the nervous shoulders, the thin, creative wrists, the unprecedented sculpture of the temples and eye-sockets. I see her grave and introspective, or in such a paroxysm of laughter that the tears came into her eyes. But her eyes are shut, and I shall never see her again.

NOTES

William Charles Franklyn Plomer (1903–73), poet, short-story writer, literary consultant, reviewer and librettist to Benjamin Britten. Born in South Africa, Plomer lived in England after 1929, moving on the fringes of the Bloomsbury Group and establishing himself in the literary world.

1. Lady Oxford's autobiographical writings include *Autobiography*, (2 vols, 1920/22), *Places and Persons* (1925), *More Memories* (1933); Dame Ethel Smyth's *Impressions That Remained*, (2 vols, 1919), *Streaks of Life* (1921), *A Final Burning of Boats* (1928) and *What Happened Next* (1940). For information about Lady Oxford, see p. 178.

'A dazzling yet shy woman'*

MARGUERITE YOURCENAR

I translated into French Virginia Woolf's penultimate novel, *The Waves*, and have no regrets since ten months' work was rewarded by a visit to Bloomsbury and two brief hours with a dazzling yet shy woman who received me in a dusk-filled room.[1] One is always wrong about the writers of one's own time, either over-estimating or denigrating them. However, I don't believe myself wrong in placing Virginia Woolf among the four or five great virtuosi of the English language and among the few contemporary novelists whose work has a chance of lasting more than ten years. And, despite many signs to the contrary, I hope that in 2500 there will still be sensibilities fine enough to appreciate the subtleties of her art.

Why do I, today, think particularly about that short, little known book that Virginia Woolf published in 1930 – *Street Haunting* (a title one might translate, not too inexactly, as *Le Rôdeur des rues de Londres*)?[2] It engages us in a swift but in no way confused flow of images, feelings and memories that overtake the mind of someone walking whilst on the self-imposed task of buying a pencil, a long, wandering peregrination of the streets of a great city, magically painted by lights and the coming dusk. Is not this thin pretext singularly Woolfian? And are not Virginia's subjects, more often than not, just her own pencils? One need remember that her art proceeds from the mystical even if she hesitates or refuses to specify this mysticism. To her, observation is more important than the object contemplated, and in the to-and-fro between the inner and outer worlds that constitutes all her books things end by appearing strangely irritating, laces when meditation threatens her frail neck with strangulation, as mirrors announce the soul. One might make of the universe a very different image of that emotional impressionism. But it is no less true that the writer of

---

* 'Une femme étincelante et timide', *Adam International Review*, nos 364–6 (1972) pp. 16–17. Translated by J. H. Stape and Raymond Gauthier.

The Waves has known how to preserve under the multiform, anxious and delicate sensations that pass a limpid clarity whose formal equivalent is serenity. In such a way, rivers receive from objects a completely superficial and ever-fleeing image that disturbs neither the transparency of their depth nor the music of their slow voyage to the sea.

'The eye is not a miner', says Virginia Woolf, 'not a diver, not a seeker after buried treasure. It floats us smoothly down a stream'.[3] If one were to classify poets by the quality of their sight, one would discover that Woolf's definition applies especially to herself. Balzac's untiring eye is a seeker after buried treasure. One could mention too Goethe's mirror-eye and, not irreverently, evoke the phases of a lighthouse in Hugo's, compare the fine eyes of Rilke, Novalis or Keats to the magic and tremulousness of the stars. In Virginia Woolf one observes an altogether different and perhaps a rarer phenomenon: one sees the eye itself, as natural as a corolla, dilating and retracting in turn, like a heart. And when I think of the martyrdom that creative work is for every great artist and of the remarkable number of new images English literature owes to Virginia Woolf, I can't but think of St Lucy of Syracuse, who gave her eyes – her two wonderful eyes – as a gift to the blind of her native island.

NOTES

Marguerite Yourcenar, pen name of Marguerite de Crayencour (1903–87), French novelist who, after 1940, made her home in the United States. She was the first woman elected to the French Academy.

1. Yourcenar's translation was published in 1937. The visit with Woolf occurred on 23 February 1937 (see *Diary*, V, 60–1).
2. First published in the *Yale Review* and then as a pamphlet (in the US only) in 1930, the piece was later reprinted in *The Death of the Moth and Other Essays* (1942).
3. 'Street Haunting: A London Adventure'. Yourcenar's version reads: 'L'oeil n'est pas un mineur, ce n'est pas non plus un plongeur, ni un chercheur de trésors cachés. L'oeil flotte mollement au gré du fleuve.'

Virginia Woolf: Writer and Personality*

LEONARD WOOLF

All human beings are extremely complicated. Virginia Woolf was one of the few people I have ever met who I think was a genius, and geniuses are slightly more complicated than ordinary people. I have myself met two people whom you have to call geniuses; one was G. E. Moore the philosopher, and the other was my wife. Her mind acted in a way in which ordinary people, who are not geniuses, never let their minds run. She had a perfectly ordinary way of thinking and talking and looking at things and living; but she also at moments had a sight of things which does not seem to me to be exactly the ordinary way in which ordinary people think and let their minds go. It was partly imagination, and it worked in ordinary life in exactly the same way every now and then as it worked in her books. She would be describing what she had seen in the street, for instance, or what someone had said to her, and then go on to weave a character of the person and everything connected with them, and it would be quite amusing. Then suddenly it would become something entirely different. I always called it leaving the ground. She would weave not the sort of scene or conversation which one felt was what anyone else would have seen and described, but something entirely different. It was often extraordinarily amusing, but in a very peculiar way – almost like a fantasy, and sometimes it was extremely beautiful. In her diary, when she describes how she wrote the last page of *The Waves,* she says that suddenly, as she was writing, the pen as it were took control of her and her thoughts raced ahead of herself, and she followed her own thoughts.[1] I think that exactly describes a genius's method of composition and imagination as opposed to that of a non-genius.

* *Listener*, 4 March 1965, pp. 327–8.

She spoke somewhere about 'the voices that fly ahead', and she followed them. She had also, and this is an important thing to remember, an insane period in her life. She had three mental breakdowns. Then, when she was at her worst and her mind was completely breaking down again the voices flew ahead of her thoughts: and she actually heard voices which were not her voice; for instance, she thought she heard the sparrows outside the window talking Greek. When that happened to her, in one of her attacks, she became incoherent because what she was hearing and the thoughts flying ahead of her became completely disconnected. Of course, people have said, from the time of the Greeks, that insanity and genius are closely allied. In my wife's case, I think one could see clearly that the two things were not disconnected.

There was a side of her which was completely like ordinary people. She liked eating and talking and going for walks, and she was fond of playing bowls and listening to music. One critic has said that she was completely withdrawn from the world and had no contact with ordinary people, but that was entirely untrue; she loved society, she loved parties, she would spend hours talking to people and would have liked to go out to parties or to theatres or to concerts every day of her life. But she had to be careful not to overtire herself, and therefore it was a perpetual struggle for her to prevent herself going into society. I have never known anyone more social with every kind of person, and the less intellectual they were, the more she liked, in a way, talking to them, because she was interested in what was going on in a person's mind. She got on extremely well with children; you cannot do that if you are withdrawn or if you do not have one side of you which is an ordinary person.

She had a very regular routine: it was dominated by her writing because writing was the most important thing to her and everything had to be regularized for it. Her day began after breakfast, at about half-past nine, when she went into her work-room, which was a very peculiar room. When we lived in Tavistock Square there was an enormous room which had been a billiards room, I imagine, and there she sat in an armchair, in the most frightful disorder – almost squalor – because the Hogarth Press's publishing business which we had started used it as a storeroom for the books, and she was by no means a tidy writer, or tidy with papers. There she would write with a pen and ink on a board on her lap for the morning; if she was well, she would probably write for two or three hours, but whenever she was at all ill, she had to be very careful not to overwork and sometimes was allowed to write only for an hour a day. Then she had lunch, and then she almost always went for a walk; she was very fond of walking about the London streets and observing things, just letting the impact of what she saw come upon her. I think her writing in her books is extraordinarily visual.

She was the most conscientious writer that I have ever known. Even where the voices flew ahead of her and the pen followed her thoughts, thoughts actually controlling her, written at the most tremendous pace, that was not the final version; sometimes she would go on for five or six revisions.

She always said that she had no education at all, and was rather pleased at the thought. It was not really true; she never went to school, I think partly because she was very delicate as a child, but her father, Sir Leslie Stephen, was a literary man of the first water – a Victorian of the Victorians. He was the editor of the *Dictionary of National Biography*; he was a very good essayist; he edited one of the quarterlies.[2] He had a very good library of all the great English writers. His daughter, Virginia, was given the run of it, at an early age, and he would discuss with her afterwards what she had read. They used to go for walks in Kensington Gardens, and he would talk about what the children were reading and the people he had known. He married as his first wife Thackeray's daughter; she died, but the other daughter, Lady Ritchie, who had married Sir Richmond Ritchie, was a writer of some genius and very fond of my wife.[3] She had met every conceivable person, from Charlotte Brontë downwards, and had written the most fascinating descriptions of them. Therefore, in a way, my wife was born into English literature.

She must have begun to write fairly early, but I have not found anything written by her much before 1900, when she was eighteen.[4] She began by writing diaries. Then she taught herself to write by writing, which is, I imagine, the only way in which one can. She began writing for a paper called *The Speaker*. Then *The Times Literary Supplement* was started, and Richmond, the editor, knew the Stephen family.[5] At any rate, she became one of his most cherished reviewers. Then when she was about twenty-five, she began writing a novel, *The Voyage Out*, but she re-wrote it, I think, seven times from end to end. I don't think one could possibly know that: the book reads as if it had just been written straight out. But she found in an old cupboard once five or six complete versions of *The Voyage Out* and burnt them.

She always got into a terrible state about a book when she had finished it. In fact, it was always one of the dangerous times for her health because the strain was terrific. When she finished *The Years*, which was one of the most popular of her novels, she thought it was hopelessly bad and got into such a state about it that we decided that she would have to stop thinking about it, and we went away and she put it out of her mind. Then she came back and started on it again and she cut out an enormous chunk in the middle. That is the only time in which she ever scrapped anything entirely.

She wrote *Orlando* as a sort of joke, and therefore was not worried about it as she was so much by other novels. If you write that kind of farce, I suppose it is easier to write, but I am quite certain that she enjoyed writing her novels immensely; it was her greatest pleasure in life. But she was hopelessly sensitive about everything, particularly about writing. Any criticism or feeling that the thing was not right was almost torture. I certainly have never felt about anything in the world anything like what she felt about the slightest thing wrong with anything she had written. Therefore, although the actual writing was of enormous importance to her, there was also this torture of having to get it right in the end.

It is difficult to know whether she knew exactly what her position was as a writer. She knew that she had reached a very high position among contemporary writers. I don't think she really very much worried about that; but any individual criticism or any unpleasant thing said about her as a writer, she minded very much indeed.

I think myself that *The Waves* is a great book and has all the marks of great literature. Whether any of the others are on the same level I rather doubt. *To the Lighthouse* is probably a great novel; I don't think the others are on the same level. What I mean by a great novel is that it is on the same level as, say, a book by Charlotte Brontë or even George Eliot or even probably *Wuthering Heights*. I don't think one should say more than that. Also, as a critic, I think she was very good.

NOTES

Leonard Sidney Woolf (1880–1969), political theorist, journalist, novelist, editor and publisher. An Apostle at Cambridge, he became acquainted there with Thoby Stephen and a number of the men who were later members of the Bloomsbury Group. After seven years in Ceylon, he returned to England on home leave, resigning his civil service post to marry Virginia Stephen in August 1912.

1. See entry of 7 February 1931, *Diary*, IV, 10.
2. Stephen edited the prestigious *Cornhill Magazine* from 1871 to 1882.
3. Harriet Marian Thackeray (1840–75), younger daughter of the major Victorian novelist William Makepeace Thackeray. Anne Isabelle Thackeray Ritchie (1837–1919), memoirist and novelist, the model for *Night and Day*'s Mrs Hilbery. Sir Richmond Thackeray Willoughby Ritchie (1854–1912; knighted 1907), civil servant.
4. As a child Woolf had written for the family newspaper, *The Hyde Park Gate News* (see p. 7). See also Woolf's *A Passionate Apprentice: The Early Journals: 1897–1909*, ed. Mitchell A. Leaska (London: Hogarth Press, 1990).
5. Bruce Lyttelton Richmond (1871–1964; knighted 1935), editor of *The Times Literary Supplement* (established 1902).

Virginia Woolf: A Portrait*

DAVID GARNETT

Virginia Woolf's father, Leslie Stephen, came of a family famous already in law and politics: particularly famous for the part its members played in the agitation against the slave trade. He added lustre to the family record, resigning a fellowship at Cambridge University because he was not prepared to take Holy Orders as a clergyman – which was then expected – as he realised that he was an agnostic (he himself coined the word), that is, he held an open mind with suspended belief on religious matters. On leaving the university he devoted himself to criticism and to literature. His first marriage, to Thackeray's daughter, was unhappy. She suffered from recurring fits of insanity.

---

* 'Virginia Woolf', *Great Friends: Portraits of Seventeen Writers* (London: Macmillan, 1979; New York: Atheneum, 1980) pp. 114, 116–30.

After her death he married one of the most beautiful women in England, Mrs Julia Duckworth, who had been left a widow with two sons and one daughter. By her he had two sons and two daughters. They grew up in a large house in London, spending their holidays in Cornwall, surrounded by famous men and women, the friends of their parents. James Russell Lowell – then American Ambassador – was, as his letters show, not only a close friend and admirer of Leslie Stephen but for many years, until his death, the devoted friend of Julia. Henry James was a frequent visitor to the Stephen houses in London and in Cornwall. George Meredith was an equally close friend.[1] The painter Watts, who had known Julia from a young girl, was a friend who painted their portraits; that of Leslie Stephen is good. That of Julia gives less idea of her beauty than the photographs taken by the pioneer photographer, her aunt, Mrs Cameron.[2] But besides this background of culture and high thinking, there was a worldly element brought in partly by the Duckworth boys,[3] partly by Stephen's eminence and Julia's beauty.

Mrs Cornish, who was famous for her directness, once came into a room where all the men were grouped round Julia Stephen and paying little attention to anyone else. Mrs Cornish looked at Julia, nodded her head and remarked, 'What a killjoy!'

The background of the Stephen household is resurrected by Virginia in her novel, *To the Lighthouse*. But Julia died when Virginia was fourteen, and she grew up in the shadow of her eminent, querulous father, reading every book she would lay hands on, and trying to learn Greek by herself.

The Duckworth boys, grown up into smart worldly young men, did their utmost to bring their half-sisters out into society, and to arrange good marriages for them. Defeated by Vanessa after terrible scenes, George Duckworth turned to his younger sister. If Duncan Grant is to be believed, Virginia, in spite of her beauty, must have been unpromising material. Duncan wrote: 'Upon an unforeseen introduction, for instance, there was an expression of blazing defiance, a few carefully chosen banalities, and a feeling of awkwardness'.[4]

But even after the most ludicrous social disasters, George would slip into her bedroom, clasp Virginia in his arms and whisper 'Beloved'. The poor fellow not only felt it his sacred duty to marry his sisters to titled husbands, but was in love with them himself. It was natural enough: they were outstandingly beautiful, and he seemed incapable of realising their dislike of his embraces, as well as for all he stood for.

What follows is an escape story. But without Vanessa to organise their escape, and their brother Thoby to introduce Leonard Woolf and his friends from Cambridge, George Duckworth might have driven Virginia into an asylum for the whole of her life. As it was he did harm enough.

It was possible to escape from a half-brother: it might not have been from parents. If they had not lost both their parents early in life, the greatest English woman painter and the greatest woman writer of the first half of the twentieth century would have probably made 'good' marriages, and their work would have been that of amateurs. Mrs Cornish called their mother a 'killjoy' perhaps not only because her beauty attracted all the men, but because she was gloomy, serious, devoted to good works, and was, except for her agnosticism, a conventional Victorian lady. If she had lived, Vanessa would have wasted hours in soup-kitchens which were better spent at her easel, and Virginia, married to some handsome young peer, would have ruined his life and done little else.

After Leslie Stephen's death Vanessa organised their escape, and they took a house, 46 Gordon Square, which they shared with their real brothers, Thoby and the youngest, Adrian. Then, after Thoby's death, Vanessa married his great friend, Clive Bell, and Virginia and Adrian went to live in Fitzroy Square. The spare rooms in both houses were often occupied by Thoby's friends from Cambridge; Bloomsbury had begun.

Shortly after their escape, Virginia burned her boats by taking part in the famous *Dreadnought* hoax got up by her brother Adrian. Anyone, or any institution that was pompous or took itself seriously, appealed to his sense of humour. 'The Establishment', to use a modernism, was fair game. Virginia in a burst of defiance took a leading part in the brilliantly successful practical joke. A telegram purporting to be from the Foreign Office was sent to the Admiral on board the *Dreadnought*, then the largest battleship in the world, saying that the Crown Prince of Abyssinia was coming down to look over the *Dreadnought*, and the Admiral was asked to show him every courtesy. Virginia was disguised as the Crown Prince, Adrian a supposed interpreter, Duncan Grant a member of the Prince's suite, Horace Cole an official from the Foreign Office.

The practical joke caused a furore. It was a mere escapade and flouting of authority, but it was the kind of escapade that Victorian dowagers were not willing to condone.

The liberation they had sought was complete, and it went a long way. One day, when Virginia and Vanessa were alone, 'the door opened and the long and sinister figure of Mr Lytton Strachey stood on the threshold. He pointed his finger at a stain on Vanessa's white dress. "Semen?" he said. Can one really say it? I thought and we burst out laughing. With that one word all barriers of reticence and reserve went down'.[5]

That quotation from a paper Virginia read to the Memoir Club shows that the Stephen sisters were unusual young women.

The so-called Bloomsbury circle, of which its members were never conscious, owed its existence to them. They had inherited all of their mother's beauty and their father's clear-minded intelligence. No man, however intelligent or free-spoken, had to adapt his lightest conversation, or most serious discussions in an argument, to their presence. They were fully the equals in wit and in wisdom and originality of mind of the men around them: Lytton Strachey, Clive Bell, Desmond MacCarthy, Morgan Forster and Leonard Woolf.

The latter had been a close friend at Cambridge of Lytton Strachey, and had then spent seven years as a British administrator in Ceylon. He had won golden opinions from his superiors, and there is little doubt that he had been marked out as a future Governor of Ceylon. But during his leave he fell passionately in love with Virginia and resigned his job in the hope that she would marry him. Two years before the 1914–18 War, she finally did.

Although they were devoted to each other, and Virginia was indeed in many ways dependent on Leonard's moral support, the marriage was clouded by Virginia's recurrent fits of insanity. These were connected with her writing, and were liable to come on after the strain of finishing one of her novels. During one of these lapses she heard the birds in the trees singing in Greek; sometimes she was violent. Leonard was forever on the watch and by keeping her from overworking, or going to too many parties – which she loved – he was able to ward off these attacks. I never saw any traces of madness in her, but I think her genius owed much to her nervous instability, and that her wildly poetical imagination was often only just this side of the borderline.

I first saw Virginia while she was still the fierce creature that

Duncan describes. It was at a fancy-dress ball in aid of Women's Suffrage at Crosby Hall very soon after it had been re-erected in Cheyne Walk. Wagner was the greatest of musicians then, and all the cultured who could afford it went to hear *The Ring* at Bayreuth. So Virginia was dressed as a Valkyrie. She was very slim and astonishingly beautiful as she stood at gaze near me and Adrian, who was already a friend of mine.

Then she caught sight of a female friend on the other side of the ballroom and swooped on her like a falcon.

She was then at work on her first novel, *The Voyage Out*, which was accepted for publication by her half-brother Gerald Duckworth. She married Leonard Woolf in August 1912. Her health went up and down. Then a year later she had to enter a nursing home. It was partly to give Virginia an unexciting occupation, partly in order to print and publish, that Leonard bought a printing press so that she could set up her own stories. Such experimental writings would not have found a publisher in the first war. Thus the Hogarth Press came into existence, named after their house in Richmond. It was not until 1924 that they moved to 52 Tavistock Square, just round the corner from where their closest friends and relatives were living. Her niece, Angelica,[6] wrote this description of Virginia there:

> She was the most enchanting aunt that anyone is ever likely to have.... To start with there was her beauty, her rare and special physical beauty which reminded one of the most aristocratic and nervous of racehorses or greyhounds and which fascinated me and possessed me even as a child. Her face with its vulnerable narrow temples and deeply hooded grey-green eyes shutting at an unexpected moment like the eyes of a bird and then opening to pierce me with a glance of amused intelligence. Above all her sensitive and sardonic mouth with a very pronounced downward curve, expressive often of the most intense amusement. Then her gestures which were somewhat jerky, her long hands waving a still longer cigarette-holder. She would puff the smoke out of the corner of her mouth and chuckle at some secret and intimate joke that we shared between us.
>
> I remember going round to have tea with her at No. 52 Tavistock Square. I would climb the rather bleak stone stairs and be let in by the maid half-way up, and when at last at the top, Virginia would be there to welcome me, longlegged, longfingered, and with silver hair escaping about her head....

Leonard would come up from the cellar in which was the office of the Hogarth Press and have tea with us ... and Virginia would call him Leo, almost as though she were trying to make me think of him as a noble lion with a mane and then she would banter him through me. 'What shall we make old Leo tell us about?' she would say. 'Has he caught many mice today in the cellar?' Leonard would take very little notice of this sort of affectionate and whimsical baiting. He would turn and look at me with the bluest of blue eyes fringed with the blackest of lashes and start on some different subject. It made me feel like an eaglet in its nest sitting between those two pairs of eyes, so different in quality – Leonard's the most intense of the two, Virginia's opening with surprise or gleaming with amusement, but each pair fastened on me with genuine and flattering interest in all my minute and childish affairs and friendships and the occurrences of daily life.

When Virginia's nephew, Julian Bell,[7] was at Cambridge he gave a picnic at Quy Fen at which she was present. My sons Richard and William were about seven and five years old, and they must have heard that 'the Woolves are coming'. After we had bathed and had our lunch, I saw the little boys scrambling away among some willow bushes and then returning to bait Virginia, who was pursuing them on all fours, growling that she was a she-wolf. I think the game may have been all the more thrilling because tinged with a touch of fear. There was just the faintest possibility that she might not be like the foster-mother of Romulus and Remus, but an actual werewolf. Her growls were convincing.

Angelica also gives a description of visiting Virginia at Monk's House, Rodmell, not far from her own home Charleston, in Sussex:

it was in the country that she seemed her happiest. Going over to tea with her at Rodmell was a constant pleasure to us during the summer holidays. Virginia would preside over the teapot in the dining-room, which was on a lower level than the garden outside. The green light filtering down through the leaves of plants pressed against the window panes intensified the feeling that she was the Queen of a translucent underwater world. But it was a world full of fun and gaiety and sparkling warmth. A great deal of teasing would go on and bursts of laughter as Virginia's flights of fancy became more and more unpredictable. After tea we swam out into the open and had a game of bowls, which we played on the Woolfs' lawn overlooked by the village church and ourselves overlooking the Ouse valley, which stretched away into the distance until it was met and bounded by Mount Caburn.

I almost always saw Leonard and Virginia together. During the war they would arrive on bicycles, Virginia a bit flushed, her eyes sparkling as she took in the faces of the company, Leonard silent, lean and mossy, greeting me very quietly, or speaking only to his spaniel to curb its demonstrations. Virginia's went uncurbed.

When I went to their house, it was Leonard who would open the door, and after his quiet greeting, I would go in and find Virginia still somewhat tempestuous and storm-tossed even in-doors. She was a sea that I never saw in a flat calm: the wind was always blowing, the waves breaking. Her mind had the same sweeping quality.

I never knew what Virginia would talk about or what she would say, but I did know what she would not. She would never make the living into the dead, or the concrete into the abstract. She would never try to harmonise or streamline her hearers' conflict-ing ideas and sense-impressions into a uniform, consistent, neutral-tinted world. She would not generalise, she would always particularise; never flatten the focus, always heighten the three-dimensional depth of detail. Her imagination ranged in a world in which everything was alive. She knew that every living thing is unique, that only when its unique quality is perceived can it be understood and become a subject for art.

It was the unlikenesses that she looked for not the likenesses. When the revelation of some unique quality in the person she was talking about, or talking to, came to her, she would stretch her neck out like a bird and crow with delighted laughter, and her voice in moments of excitement would break and split like an adolescent schoolboy's.

She was interested in everyone. She responded to young men and girls who aspired to write; she entered the make-believe worlds of children; she was fascinated by the old familiar figures of her childhood, the friends and relatives of her father's and of her girlhood, some shrivelled by time, some still brightly vigorous, some horribly decaying. She could be wittily sharp and cruel about those she disliked.

There was a strange contradiction in Virginia. She was so beautiful, so tall, so aristocratic and in many ways so fastidious. But she had a sense of humour that would stick at nothing, like Shakespeare's, or Chaucer's. And she had an appetite and a relish for life that one finds most often in market women.

Nothing made her wish to avert her eyes and cross to the other side of the street. Like Rembrandt she could have found the subject for a work of art in a side of beef.

Because of this there were no doors closed to her: she could pluck the secret from the heart of an old dried-up lawyer, a charwoman or a young actor enjoying his first triumph. Whenever Virginia appeared she brought a new treasure trove with her, something that she had heard in the street, been told over the counter, found in an old letter. After she had been to a party she would come round and regale her sister with an account of it, and what she said might have been written by Thackeray if he had been a poet with a completely uninhibited sense of humour. She was vain and sensitive to criticism, but she liked making herself into a ridiculous figure and laughing at herself.

Almost all her stories had one point, one object: to catch the unique living self that makes one human being different from another.

When she went into the street, she saw the same crowds that we all do, hurrying and scurrying along like disordered sheep. But for her the spectacle was, I think, an illusion. She never forgot that each figure was not a unit in a mass, but an individual with a secret. So that even in Oxford Street there was no crowd, and on the Downs the sheep were not a flock: the shepherd or his dog could tell each one apart.

To that I would add that as a young man I was well aware of her avidity to find out my secret feelings and of the ruthlessness with which she might use her knowledge, so for several years I was shy of her. If Mr Albee had been born to ask his question, 'Who's afraid of Virginia Woolf?'[8] I should have admitted that I was.

But as time went on I felt more sure of her. She used to call me her badger – not Bunny, as other people did – and from the way in which she asked, 'How's my old Badger? What's he been writing?' I knew that she felt an amused but warm affection for me. Then, in the year before her death, when she realised that Angelica was in love with me, her love embraced us both, and she was a most comforting support, whatever her doubts about Angelica's wisdom.

I cannot improve upon my wife's description of Virginia's physical appearance, but I would add this: that she was beautiful with
a beauty that gave the lie to Shakespeare's lament in the sonnet:

> When forty winters shall besiege thy brow
> And dig deep trenches in thy beauty's field,
> Thy youth's proud livery, so gazed on now,
> Will be a tattered weed, of small worth held.[9]

Virginia was fifty-nine at the time of her death, but the signs
of that siege, the presence of those trenches, did not subtract from
her beauty. The hollow temples, hollow hooded eyes, and almost
fleshless face were as lovely as the beauty she had as a girl in
her twenties when I first remember her.

Virginia committed suicide. The war horrified her, and the sky
in Sussex was often full of fighting aircraft. She felt madness coming
on and found death in the river. Angelica and I had seen her
two days before, and she had never been warmer, or expressed
her love for us more freely.

Dogmatising about the sexes is foolish. I only hazard a suggestion here because it may explain a quality in Virginia Woolf's
work. For she made what men regard as a weakness in women's
minds, her strength. Her originality as a writer was largely in
expressing it. Women, it is said, do not concentrate. They can
attend to the subject in hand, but their attention has not the whole-
heartedness of a man's. If so, it is just possible that since women
have been cooking the supper, mending clothes, listening to half-
a-dozen children all talking at once, and keeping them good-tem-
pered and amused since before the dawn of history, they have
learned to be able to attend to several things at a time. A man,
on the other hand, focuses his mind. A watch has stopped, let us
say. Time and space and his environment cease to exist for him
when he begins taking it to pieces and analysing the possible
reasons for it going wrong.

In art and literature men do the same. They concentrate on one
point after another, and the result is a series of events or facts or
statements, logically related together, on which the mind is focused,
as our eyes are focused on the illuminated patch of road when
we drive at night. We do not see what is in the woods or fields
on either side of the road. Almost all women writers have imi-
tated men more or less successfully in this. But Virginia Woolf's

work resembles that of the woman who is mending clothes in the kitchen while she watches pots simmering on the stove and tells a story to the children around her knee without forgetting that there is a home-made cake in the oven which, judging from the smell, will soon be ready to come out.

In other words, time, space and the environment never cease to exist for Virginia. One of her chief interests, or at any rate one of the things she is always aware of, is relative motion.

> But there was no silence; all the time the motor omnibuses were turning their wheels and changing their gear; like a vast nest of Chinese boxes all of wrought steel turning ceaselessly one within another the city murmured; on the top of which the voices cried aloud and the petals of myriads of flowers flashed their colours into the air.

That last sentence of the little sketch 'Kew Gardens', written towards the end of the First World War, illustrates a preoccupation of Virginia's mind. All her subsequent novels and stories show the same absorbed interest in, and awareness of, simultaneously motions which are independent of each other. It was by the means of that awareness that she developed her very individual method of telling her stories and exhibiting her characters to the reader.

Jacob in *Jacob's Room* is shown to us as a young man through the eyes of old Mrs Norman protesting feebly as he enters the railway compartment, 'This is not a smoking-carriage' and imagining that she would throw her scent bottle with her right hand, and tug the communication cord with her left, if he assaulted her. 'She was fifty years of age, and had a son at college. Nevertheless, it is a fact that men are dangerous'. She sees his face and is reassured. We see Jacob through her eyes as he travels to Cambridge, then as she gets out: 'this sight of her fellow-traveller was completely lost in her mind, as the crooked pin dropped by a child into the wishing-well twirls in the water and disappears for ever'.[10]

That image is an illustration of Virginia Woolf's other most remarkable quality as a writer. The prose is like poetry. The language is as sensitive to the beauty of things as the writer is to the multiplicity of events. The dispersion of attention that might have become a trick is never so in her. It is never a formula, but the expression of her individual taste and as carefully chosen, as inevitable, as her taste in words. In Bloomsbury we were all living very much in a world of painters, looking at pictures all the time, and listening to discussions which were always devoted to the visual arts rather than to literature. Indeed for many years I was accustomed to hear the adjective 'literary' used only as a term of abuse. I think Virginia learned something about her art from the painters and art critics, from watching her sister Vanessa and Duncan Grant paint, from listening to Roger Fry and Clive Bell. The latter greatly encouraged her when she was writing her first novel.

Some critics have been rash enough to say that Virginia Woolf drew not only the theme of *Mrs Dalloway* from James Joyce's *Ulysses* but her literary method as well. I don't believe they know what the theme of *Mrs Dalloway* is. And as for literary method! *Mrs Dalloway* derives directly from *Jacob's Room* in method. And the origin of *Jacob's Room* was, as we know from Virginia's diary, her experiments in writing, 'The Mark on the Wall' and 'Kew Gardens' which, she said, shake hands and dance.[11]

'The Mark on the Wall' was published in 1917, and 'Kew Gardens' set up in type and published in 1919 – the year in which she read the first excerpts from *Ulysses* in the *Little Review*.

Not that there are no literary influences. If, as Angelica suggested, she Virginia were a racehorse, I should expect to find Laurence Sterne and Henry James in her pedigree. The opening chapters of *Night and Day* have a distinct flavour of James. Later on, though the texture of her writing is quite unlike that of Henry James, there is the same kind of sensitive analysis characteristic of the novels of James's middle period. On her writing-table at Asheham she kept a framed and autographed photograph of Henry James. And surely anyone can see in the wilful interruption of the narrative, which turns out to be so relevant to the matter in hand, an echo of *Tristram Shandy*?

The theme of *Mrs Dalloway* is probably more easily missed by the younger generation and by foreigners than by those who grew up surrounded by the English social scene before the first war. The theme of *Mrs Dalloway* is the death of the soul, or perhaps one should say the withering, for death is an exaggeration. It is the study of a woman who as a girl had her chance but took the wrong turning, who failed to realise her highest potentialities by timidly sticking to the traditions of her class.

Peter Walsh, who had been in love with her, puts it clearly:

> There was always something cold in Clarissa, he thought. She had always, even as a girl, a sort of timidity, which in middle age becomes conventionality, and then it's all up, it's all up, he thought, looking rather drearily into the glassy depths, and wondering whether by calling at that hour he had annoyed her.[12]

And it is Peter Walsh, who waking suddenly after dozing in the park, puts a name to it by exclaiming: 'the death of the soul'. Now whatever the theme of Joyce's *Ulysses* may be, it certainly is not the death of the soul resulting from too rigid an adherence to the conventions and too great a love of social success and of respectability. Clarissa Dalloway took the wrong turning when she was a girl. Her gay, irresponsible friend Sally, and Peter Walsh, who awakened her mind, but whom she rejected, represent the intellectual who values personal freedom and spontaneity and truth above social and monetary success – that is to say – Virginia Woolf's world, which she, and her sister Vanessa Stephen, very definitely chose, in opposition to the world of her half-brothers, the Duckworths. Peter Walsh indeed has the independence of mind of Leonard Woolf, although Peter is not as intelligent as Leonard, nor is he a Jew. And the novel, which is an account of a day in the life of Mrs Dalloway, is an analysis of just how and why she had failed to live up to the hopes of two most intimate friends, who had chosen freedom. It was partly cowardice in her, but perhaps also a certain idealistic loyalty to the traditions of her class. This is shown by her admiration for Lady Bexborough who had been billed to open some charity, and who carried out her engagement while she held in her hand the telegram which had that moment reached her, announcing her son's death in battle. *Noblesse oblige*. One may be appalled and horrified by some examples of the tradition of *noblesse oblige*. One may regard it as inhuman, but one respects it. And *noblesse oblige* is deep, deep in what are still the British upper classes. Politically it is something of immense value: a fascist leader like General Franco, a civil war like that in Spain, have been unthinkable in England because the tradition of *noblesse oblige* forbids them.

The comic side, the contemptible side of Mrs Dalloway's world is represented by Hugh Whitbread who has a job at court 'blacking the King's boots', his friends say unkindly. But all the same in spite of his greediness, snobbishness, fatness and general imbecility, Virginia has a sneaking liking for him because he is a gentleman and invariably considerate of other people's feelings, although of course he doesn't know what they are.

Clarissa Dalloway goes out shopping, meets her friends, returns home a little embittered because her husband has been asked to lunch without her, although it was only to meet Hugh Whitbread, who is helping Lady Bruton to write a letter to *The Times*.

Peter Walsh has come back that day from India, just as Leonard Woolf had returned from Ceylon. He is invited to Clarissa Dalloway's party that evening, preparations for which have already disorganised her household.

Virginia gives a perfectly astonishing picture of the surface of London as it was in the early twenties. The spirit of the West End of fashionable London glittering during the season in June has never been brought so well between the covers of a book. The prose descriptions are full of poetry; no one else's prose is so full of poetry. Even the clouds sailing overhead are not forgotten:

A puff of wind (in spite of the heat, there was quite a wind) blew a thin black veil over the sun and over the Strand. The faces faded; the omnibuses suddenly lost their glow. For although the clouds were of mountainous white so that one could fancy hacking hard chips off with a hatchet, with broad golden slopes, lawns of celestial pleasure gardens, on their flanks, and had all the appearance of settled habitations assembled for the conference of gods above the world, there was a perpetual movement among them. Signs were interchanged, when, as if to fulfil some scheme arranged already, now a summit dwindled, now a whole block of pyramidal size which had kept its station inalterably advanced into the midst or gravely led the procession to fresh anchorage. Fixed as they seemed at their posts, at rest in perfect unanimity, nothing could be fresher, freer, more sensitive superficially than the snow-white or gold-kindled surface; to change, to go, to dismantle the solemn assemblage was immediately possible; and in spite of the grave fixity, the accumulated robustness and solidity, now they struck light to the earth, now darkness.

And then she introduces what at first sight appears to be a complete irrelevance – the study of Septimus Smith and his Italian

wife. Septimus has fought in the war and delayed shell-shock
has resulted in madness. His delusions are drawn from personal
experience:

> Men must not cut down trees. There is a God. (He noted
> such revelations on the backs of envelopes.) Change the world.
> No one kills from hatred. Make it known (he wrote it down).
> He waited. He listened. A sparrow perched on the railing op-
> posite chirped Septimus, Septimus, four or five times over and
> went on, drawing its notes out, to sing freshly and piercingly
> in Greek words how there is no crime and, joined by another
> sparrow, they sang in voices prolonged and piercing in Greek
> words, from trees in the meadow of life beyond a river where
> the dead walk, how there is no death.
>   There was his hand; there the dead. White things were as-
> sembling behind the railings opposite. But he dared not look.
> Evans was behind the railings!

She is drawing madness from the inside. But what is Septimus
doing in the book? What relation has he to Mrs Dalloway? I think
that he is the shadow that throws the brilliant colours into relief.
He is the reminder of what is just round the corner for each of us:
madness, tragedy, death. Septimus and his unhappy wife deepen
the book and add greatly to it. They are not irrelevant, for they are
always there among us. We are aware of their tragedy during all
the preparations for the party, and when Septimus throws himself
out of a window to his death we meet the specialist who has attended him and had arranged to send him away from his wife to
an asylum, at Clarissa Dalloway's party in his white tie and tails.

Then there is another strand: Clarissa's daughter, Elizabeth, who
is challenging and questioning her mother's values, accepting for
the moment those of her ugly, unattractive history teacher, Miss
Kilman. One is confident that Elizabeth will find something very
much better before long, but even Miss Kilman is better than
unquestioning acceptance. Elizabeth is just at the age when a young
girl often resents the fact that she is bound to grow into a woman:

> And already, even as she stood there, in her very well-cut clothes,
> it was beginning... People were beginning to compare her to
> poplar trees, early dawn, hyacinths, fawns, running water, and
> garden lilies; and it made her life a burden to her, for she so

much preferred being left alone to do what she liked in the country, but they would compare her to lilies, and she had to go to parties, and London was so dreary compared with being alone in the country with her father and the dogs.

Finally there is the party – the party that brings all the strands together and that symbolises all that Clarissa Dalloway values. Sally Seton whom we have only known from memories in the minds of Clarissa Dalloway and Peter Walsh, and who broke away from her family and said outrageous things that shocked the conventions of her youth, sweeps in uninvited. She has scarcely had time to embrace her hostess when the Prime Minister is announced and Clarissa has to leave her old friend, and Sally finds Peter Walsh. They talk about their hostess as Clarissa takes the Prime Minister around. Sally condemns her utterly:

> What Sally felt was simply this. She had owed Clarissa an enormous amount. They had been friends, not acquaintances, friends, and she still saw Clarissa all in white going about the house with her hands full of flowers – to this day tobacco plants made her think of Bourton. But – did Peter understand? – she lacked something. Lacked what was it? She had charm; she had extraordinary charm. But ... married Richard Dalloway? a sportsman, a man who cared only for dogs. Literally, when he came into the room he smelt of the stables. And then all this? She waved her hand.
> ... Clarissa was at heart a snob – one had to admit it, a snob. And it was that that was between them, she was convinced. Clarissa thought she had married beneath her, her husband being – she was proud of it – a miner's son. Every penny they had he had earned.

But Peter is bored by this and is seduced by the charm of Clarissa's personality into accepting her as she is.

That is my reading of this wonderful book which seems to me to be one of the great novels in the English language. The subject of it, I believe, had been suggested by what happened to a close friend of her girlhood who as they say had made 'a very suitable marriage' such as George Duckworth wanted for his sisters. But thanks largely to Vanessa and to Thoby, she had escaped to freedom and a very different marriage.

Many critics rank *To the Lighthouse* above *Mrs Dalloway* as the greatest of Virginia's novels. I do not, for the theme of her own parents and childhood seems to me less important. The characterisation may go deeper, but Mrs Dalloway is not only a social indictment it is an interweaving in presentation which as far as I know, is unique in literature. With these two masterpieces, the critics respectfully place *The Waves* and *The Years*. But again I differ. I turn back on the judgment of the thoughtful reasonable man who asks that the novel should comment with a certain realism upon life as we live it.

There is more to great writing – great prose writing, great storytelling, than that. There are fantasy and inspiration which rank with great poetry. Many writers have had glimpses of this (myself included) standing like urchins peeping through into the Great Top of the circus, into fairyland. Virginia is the greatest of the fantasists of our time. I am carried away by *Orlando*. It is, I think, the essence of Virginia herself. She started it as a joke, and this gave her a freedom that enraptures me. *Orlando* is also a love-letter. It has a gay teasing intimacy which puts it above that other work of fantasy, *Flush*. I love *Flush* and was lucky enough to be able to write a review of it which drew the following letter from Virginia:[13]

52 Tavistock Sq
Sunday
Private

My dear Bunny,
    You were more than generous and wholly delightful about *Flush* and Virginia last week; and I had meant to write and thank you before, but being altogether a dog, as you justly observe, had no time to go to The London Library and prove that I'm not so inaccurate as you think. No. I'm rather proud of my facts. About license, for instance; surely I made it plain that I was referring to nature, not the post office? license natural to his age – well, I ask you what has that license got to do with the Encyclopaedia? or the Post Office, or six and eightpence? Natures license, sometimes called lust. About the working mans cottage; I agree it looks like a farm in the picture; but Mr Orion Horne calls it a working mans cottage; and he saw it; and was not a picturesque artist.[14] Painters at that date always enlarge

houses out of consideration for their owners. Such is my view as a biographer (and oh lord how does any one pretend to be a biographer?) As for asphalt, I admit I have my doubts; but I suspect that the Prince Regent liked asphalt – asphalt seems to me implied by the Pavilion. But how could you let slip the horrid anachronism which stares at you, bright red, on page I don't know what? There were no pillar boxes in the year 1846. They were invented by Anthony Trollope about 1852.[15] Don't expose me. If you do, my sales will prick like a bubble. Old gentlemen will die in fury. I could go on, but will stop, having I hope partly vindicated my claim to truth speaking. Yes, the last paragraph as originally written was simply Queen Victoria dying all over again – Flush remembered his entire past in Lytton's best manner; but I cut it out, when he was not there to see the joke.[16] But what a good critic you are – lots of things you said I think of in the watches of the night; they stick like burs; whereas the others, save Desmond's, run off my coat like water.[17]

Your affectionate old English springer spaniel Virginia

There was another side to Virginia as a writer. She was a literary critic of the front rank. In her two volumes, *The Common Reader* and the posthumous volume *Granite*, she shows that she was not the daughter of Leslie Stephen for nothing. Indeed she was sensitive to worlds of which he was ignorant. The wish of her godfather James Russell Lowell that her heredity might blossom and bear fruit was abundantly fulfilled. She was a scholar whose critical works reveal the balanced orderly powers of a first-rate intelligence. At any moment she could write a biographical sketch, or an article in *The Times Literary Supplement* marshalling her facts and delivering her judgement with ease and wit. In her novels and stories the originality of her approach, the beauty of her language and the associations which echo poetry like the murmur of the waves, evoked for us by a shell clasped to the ear, make Virginia one of the half-dozen great women writers, and perhaps the least like a man of all.

NOTES

David Garnett (1892–1981), novelist and bookseller, a Bloomsbury intimate. He was connected with the previous literary generation through his father Edward, a publisher's reader and editor, and his mother, Constance, a noted translator of Russian fiction. His best-known work is *Lady into Fox* (1922).

1. George Meredith (1828–1909), novelist and poet.

2. Julia Margaret Cameron, née Pattle (1815–79), pioneer portrait photographer.

3. George (1868–1934) and Gerald (1870–1937).

4. See p. 138.

5. 'Old Bloomsbury', *Moments of Being: Unpublished Writings of Virginia Woolf*, ed. Jeanne Schulkind (Brighton: Sussex University Press, 1976) p. 195.

6. For information about Angelica Garnett, see p. 172.

7. Julian Heward Bell (1908–37). A promising writer, Bell was killed in the Spanish Civil War.

8. Title of the 1962 play by the American dramatist Edward Albee.

9. Shakespeare, Sonnet 2.

10. *Jacob's Room*, ch. 3.

11. 'Whether I'm sufficiently mistress of things – that's the doubt; but conceive mark on the wall, K. G. & unwritten novel taking hands & dancing in unity', entry for 26 January 1920, *Diary*, II, 14.

12. *Mrs Dalloway* (Penguin Twentieth-Century Classics) pp. 53, 152, 26–7, 147, 207–8.

13. Letter of [8 October 1933], *Letters*, V, 231–2. Garnett's review appeared in the *New Statesman*, 7 October 1933, p. 416.

14. Richard Hengist Horne (1803–84), author of *Orion*.

15. Anthony Trollope (1815–82), novelist and career civil servant in the Post Office.

16. Strachey's *Queen Victoria* (1921) concludes with the dying queen's reveries about her life.

17. Desmond MacCarthy's review of *Flush* appeared in *The Sunday Times*, 8 October 1933, p. 6.

Part VII
Woolf Remembered

The Death of Virginia Woolf*

LOUIE MAYER, ANGELICA GARNETT and ELIZABETH BOWEN

Louie Mayer: Mrs Woolf always slept outside in the garden room. She would have the breakfast and come in and have a bath. You would think there was somebody else in the bathroom, which there wasn't – she always talked to herself. And she was on the books all the time. Very much so. But the moment she come down she was quite normal, quite back to herself again. You could always tell, I think, when she was sad because she walked about very slowly, as if she was thinking. She would bump into things, you know; she might walk up in the garden, not realise she was very near a tree or something like that.

Angelica Garnett: I don't think I had realised at all the strain she was under, and I hadn't realised – partly through being exceptionally immature, I think – the impact that that stage of the war had on her. I mean the strain of the feeling that one was going to be invaded and all that. She and Leonard had decided to blow themselves up in their garage if Hitler invaded England, you know. Quite literally. And I hadn't realised that she felt she was going to go mad again. We were living close by at the time and I saw her a few days before it happened. I realised that she was under the weather, and she made this tremendous demand for love that she was in the habit of making rather. Particularly, I think, because I was an undemonstrative child, she would quite often say: 'But, Angelica, don't you love me, don't you adore me, you hate me, you *know* you don't like me at all' – this sort of way of going on. She did it particularly on that day, and I was particularly cold and undemonstrative, and then the next thing I heard was a telephone call to say that she had drowned herself.

* *Listener*, 15 January 1970, pp. 87–8.

Louie Mayer: It was near lunch time when we discovered she was missing. I cooked her a leg of mutton and got mint sauce, which she liked very much. And I rang the bell. We used to have a bell in those days, and I used to ring it, and she would hear it in the garden room and come for lunch, and Mr Woolf would come down too. When I rang it, Mr Woolf rushed downstairs and said I must go up to the sitting-room and listen to the news because the war was very bad then, and he wanted to know what had happened, in Germany, with the war. When he got there, he must have looked on the table and seen two notes laying there. One was for him, with 'Leonard' on it, and the other was for Mrs Bell, Vanessa Bell. He picked up his and read it and rushed down and said: 'Oh Louie, which way has Mrs Woolf gone? I think she might have committed suicide'. And of course I took fright and I too rushed up the garden, but I couldn't see anything. And he said: 'No, I suppose she probably went towards the river'. They found her walking-stick there – some boys found it on the river bank.

Elizabeth Bowen: The last day I saw her when I was staying there, I remember her kneeling back on the floor. We were talking away mending a torn curtain in the house. And she sat back on her heels and put her head back in a patch of early spring sun, and laughed in this consuming, choking, delightful, hooting way. It has remained with me. So that I get a curious shock when I see people regarding her entirely as a martyr of art, or a definitely tragic sort of person, claimed by the darkness. She ended, as far as we know, in darkness, but where is she now? Nobody with that capacity for joy, I think, can be ... And it *was* joy.

NOTES

Louie Mayer (b. 1912), was the Woolfs' cook at Monk's House. She remained with Leonard Woolf until his death in 1969.

Angelica Garnett (b. 1918), the daughter of Vanessa Bell, married David Garnett. She studied acting but has pursued a career in painting, drawing and illustration. Her *Deceived with Kindness: A Bloomsbury Childhood* (1985) discusses her relations with the Bloomsbury Group.

Elizabeth Dorothea Cole Bowen (1899–1973), Anglo-Irish novelist and short-story writer.

Letters of Condolence*

SIR OSBERT SITWELL and DAME ETHEL SMYTH

I

Renishaw Hall
Renishaw
N. Sheffield
4. 4. 41.

My dear Vanessa

I don't know how to write to tell you [how] deeply I sympathize with you in your irreparable loss. My sister[1] and I have been knocked over by the sadness of it; not that we continually saw Virginia, but we had the greatest admiration for her both as a writer and a person. She was, among other things, as beautiful to look at, as her words were to read. I have never seen any one with more perfect distinction. And I know how devoted you were to each other.

It is a terrible loss for many people – even those who did not know her – perhaps especially for them ... I shall always remember that dinner of the London Group – do you remember it? – many years ago, when she was to speak.[2] I sat near her and felt such pity for her nervousness. But I might have spared myself, for she made the most triumphantly beautiful speech I have ever heard, without a trace of a tremble, on the Marriage of Poetry to Music in [the] 16–17th centuries?

What a horrible world it is, and so much worse with the loss of such a beautiful, witty, interested artist. Just at the moment when most she could not be spared.

Yrs ever,
Osbert Sitwell

* Not previously published. Letters to Vanessa Bell (Charleston Papers, The Tate Gallery).

II

Coign, Woking
Good Friday 1941

My dear Vanessa

How like dear Vita to tell you I 'might care' (!) to have a line
from you & how like you to act on the suggestion & tell one
things, even, that hurt. Rereading the last two letters I had from
her (March 1st & 11th)3 I see signs of distress & for one thing her
suggesting to come here 'any Wed in April' – which she said she
'could do now' & complaining of personal separation brought
about by the war. She had never done this before, & though of
course it made me happy, *some of the time* I said to myself 'that's
not like V!' –.

I never knew that from time to time there were 'dangerous
moments'; but seeing that she declared that in spite of taking my
advice (– i.e. 'going on' though she appeared to herself to be
inspirationless, which you know was Baudelaire's advice – also,
I believe Trollope's,) altho' she went on hopefully 'striking match
after match on the box' hoping to start a flame, & none came...
(she said). I think if I had known she had those dangerous moments I might have ventured to turn up & try to carry her off for
a day or two. But I always feared to worry Leonard. Also, in
spite of all, since (as he told me in his letter what I never realised
before) *she* had times of actually dreading the return of the malady,
I believe she chose her end wisely. This war will go on for ever
& *even* if we win very very difficult years are before us, & I think
a time will come when one will rejoice that she had the courage
to go out of the world.

Dear Vanessa – you say I may ask you anything——Well, you
know I have splendid letters – heaps of them – from her; one
about London (written in Jany) that is incomparable.4 & *if* she
kept any letters of mine (only about 6 weeks ago faced by the
collapse of Meck[lenburgh] Square she said 'O what folly to keep
letters' – (To which I replied 'I always have – & always shall)... If
however she did, particularly quite recent ones, I sh. be glad to
have any back as they will elucidate certain refs in hers.

I could as soon destroy her letters as smash up beautiful china
——I remember your saying once & my agreeing – that perhaps
'The best thing she does are her letters' & I'm going to have them

typed (as sometimes her script was cryptic) & bound.

Raymond Mortimer wrote a very dear letter asking me if I would write an 'appreciation' of her. But I had to say I *couldnt*, touched as I was at his suggesting it——Later perhaps – but my God not now.

You see it was not only (I did not tell him this!) that I loved her; it was that my life [was] literally based on her. I am devoted to perhaps 7 or 8 other people in this world – two being my sister & brother – 2 or 3 a good deal younger than me – thank God——But with her it was the constant amazing contact with a mind of genius——If I came across a curious bit of life – (or something really funny) I saved it for my next letter to her—— What makes me unhappy – (for as you know she adored 'getting a letter' –) was that all March I was really ill – & neither wrote nor explained to her I was ill. I had never let 15 days elapse without writing before. I know you know – & that was the reason you told me, that you think I made a real difference to her life. The only trouble was that Leonard didn't much like me. She always said he would if we had a chance of being together for 48 [hours]. But I rather doubt it; the *Jehovah* element was too strong! & I am bad at dealing with that. I always liked him so strongly too nevertheless!

O Vanessa I feel sure that in all of views of life she saw deeper than anyone else——(How often I have felt that) and that the day will come – but it is not possible now – when one will bless her wisdom & courage.

I hope you will let me see You again some day——

Yours ever
Ethel

NOTES

For information about Sir Osbert Sitwell and Dame Ethel Smyth, see p. 52 and p. 42, respectively.

1. Dame Edith Sitwell.
2. See pp. 51–2.
3. Letter of 12 January 1941, *Letters* VI, 459–60.
4. Letters of 1 and, in fact, 10 March 1941, *Letters*, VI, 474–5, 478.

Virginia Woolf: A Tribute*

LADY OXFORD

The first time I saw Virginia Woolf was when I went to a garden-party given by her famous father, Leslie Stephen. I knew no
one at that party, but my attention was riveted upon two beautiful young women. They were standing side by side, dressed in
white muslin, with grass-green ribands round their waists. They
wore hats like those which are worn today, bunched up with
bouquets of flowers on the crowns and tied with black velvet
bows at the back. I asked someone who they were and was told:
'They are the daughters of our host; one is called Vanessa and
the other Virginia'.

Many years passed before I saw Virginia again. I went to a
concert given at Queen's Hall. I had just published my *Autobiography* which met with universal disapproval.[1] Dame Ethel Smyth
came up to me in the interval of the music and said, 'I hope you
don't mind what the critics of your book are saying. To console
you I will tell you what Virginia Woolf said about it'. I will not
repeat the undeserved praise which Virginia Woolf had bestowed
upon my first literary attempt, as I am not writing about myself;
but I was so dazzled by what my generous friend Ethel told me
that I wrote a letter of thanks to Virginia and she invited me to
go and see her. She was even more beautiful than she was when
I saw her at her father's garden-party. She and her husband were
working in a sort of cellar. I did not realize at that time that
when you are working you do not wear pretty clothes, so I said
to her, 'Were I as beautiful as you, I would wear prettier clothes'.
She replied that she was not beautiful and had never thought
much about her appearance. This was true. No woman ever cared
less about her appearance than the beautiful Virginia. Although
the greatest of artists, she was unconcerned about herself or what
she looked like. She was entirely wrapped up in her daily work

---

* 'Mrs Virginia Woolf: Lady Oxford's Tribute', *The Times*, 9 April 1941, p. 7.

with her husband. After this visit I saw her not very frequently, but off and on, and we started a correspondence, also not very frequent. But I can truly say that our conversations and her letters to me since the war started have been my only intellectual pleasure. She was always an enchanting companion.

What was curious about Virginia was that her writing, her hand-writing, countenance, and conversation were inseparably the same: equally sensitive and equally distinguished. She smiled slowly and seldom, yet when she went out of the room she left her radiant smile with me, and nothing can ever erase it.

She had what is rare among female writers, an untouchable gift of imagination. Many authors have all the 'properties' – to use a stage expression – which go to the make-up of imagination. They can write about ghosts, cemeteries, dreams, and peculiar people. But these properties are not enough. They are not fiction – they are fancy; and, although it sounds paradoxical, they do not really leave the ground. Virginia was an uneven authoress, but at her best she always left the ground. Books like *To the Lighthouse*, *The Voyage Out*, *The Waves*, and other of her obscure works have been a constant excitement to me. They stirred my imagination, and I have read and re-read them. They lifted me into another world; a world of music, of poetry, and of mystery, which was entirely her own. They were part of her twilight mind.

When I last wrote to her I felt lonely and depressed. I told her that at one time I was arrogant enough to think that I was the hostess at the festival of life, but that now I was not even a guest, and there was no 'festival'.[2] I added that when I died I hoped that she would write my obituary notice in *The Times*, as that might make me famous.[3] She replied that all the lights of London would go out were I to die, just as surely as if the lights had been turned out in the Covent Garden Opera House. This is what I felt when I heard of the death of my lovely friend, Virginia Woolf. She was unknown to the general public. I doubt if many people have even read her books. It seems only yesterday that she wrote and talked to me. But it is always 'only yesterday' when those we love die.

NOTES

Emma Alice Margaret ('Margot') Asquith, née Tennant, Countess of Oxford and Asquith (1864–1945), memoirist. The second wife of Liberal politician H. H. Asquith (Prime Minister 1908–16), she was widely connected in political and artistic circles.

1. Published in 1920/22 in two volumes.
2. For Woolf's response, see *Letters*, VI, 405.
3. Woolf recalls the request and quotes Asquith's letter to her making it in 'Am I a Snob?', *Moments of Being: Unpublished Writings of Virginia Woolf*, ed. Jeanne Schulkind (Brighton: Sussex University Press, 1976) pp. 208–9.

In Memoriam: Virginia Woolf*

LORD DAVID CECIL

Already the critics have been busy, defining her position as a representative of her age, expounding the philosophy implicit in her work. But, whether successful or unsuccessful, those efforts seem to miss the point. After all we do not read Virginia Woolf's books for philosophy or period interest – many extremely bad books can provide us equally well with these – but because they delight us, because they are works of art. It is in the qualities that go to give her art its peculiar flavour that we must search for her significance.

It is a complex flavour. Primarily it comes from her vision of life. She shows us the world from a new angle. Like other novelists she wants to describe what she feels to be the essential truth about life, as accurately as possible. But, extremely critical and born in an age of uncertain beliefs, she did not find any of the systems, old or new, by which man has sought to impose an order on experience, corresponded with reality. She, therefore, went back to the beginning. Through the eyes of one or more of her characters, she strives to record the actual process of living, simply to trace the confused succession of impression and thought and mood,

* 'A Note on Virginia Woolf', *Time and Tide*, 17 May 1941, pp. 395–6.

as it drifts, cloud-like, across the clear mirror of consciousness. Looked at like this, the elements of life assume a new proportion. The same things do not seem of the same importance. A broken jar may fill the foreground of her canvas; a declaration of war fade into the background. She will take a chapter to describe a casual stroll in which a man feels quickened to a deeper apprehension of experience: his death she may pass over in a parenthesis. Such an angle of approach does not make for drama in the ordinary sense of the word. Her novels are not dramatic. Nor do they give much scope for character-drawing. Seen through the shifting haze of the observer's moods, character loses its clear-cut outline.

It might be expected that the effect of such books would be chaotic. Surprisingly, Virginia Woolf's picture is as shapely as Jane Austen's. For instinctively she selects for emphasis only those features of her subject which strike her as significant. All the disordered matter of experience falls into a pattern imposed by her predominant creative impulse, her sensibility to beauty. Here she differs from the other contemporary painters of the stream of consciousness. The sense of beauty, the delight in what naturally pleases senses and fancy, is for some obscure reason at a discount with them. They seek rather the curious, the sensational. Virginia Woolf luxuriates in beauty like an Elizabethan. Always she is on the look-out for it, and she can find it anywhere. The accepted beauties of art and nature from a stormy sunset to a diamond necklace, a crocus to a classical temple, she appreciates, with a peculiar power to discriminate in what the precise beauty of each consists. Equally she can detect what is beautiful in objects generally considered ugly and prosaic. Far more successfully than any professional poet has she revealed the aesthetic quality in the modern scene. In the first chapter of *Mrs Dalloway*, a summer morning in Bond Street, all buses and policemen and clamouring shoppers, is made to glow with all the splendour of a Vermeer picture. Yet it is a realistic picture. Indeed, more than in anything else, her contribution to English literature lies in her unique power to combine beauty with accuracy. Most writers who specialize in 'the beautiful', spill a golden glaze of romantic sentiment over their subject, softening its harsher features. Not so Virginia Woolf. 'How exactly like Bond Street!' we find ourselves exclaiming, 'but I never knew it was so lovely'. Her artist's eye contrives to get its effect simply by isolating those aspects of her

subject that appeal to the aesthetic sense. Even the red hands of
a woman in a flower shop are used to add a ravishing note of
colour to her composition. An amusing note too: her vision is
further saved from romantic unreality by the incessant activity of
her acute and ironical observation. However enchanted she may
be, she is always able to notice and to smile. Sensibility and intelligence mingle together in a clear stream which ripples over
the objects of her contemplation, making them gleam out with an
extraordinary brilliance and distinctness.

> Down Park Lane and Piccadilly, vans, cars, omnibuses ran along
> the streets as if the streets were slots; stopped and jerked; as if
> a puzzle were solved, and then broken, for it was the season,
> and the streets were crowded. Over Park Lane and Piccadilly
> the clouds kept their freedom, wandering fitfully, staining win-
> dows gold, daubing them black, passed and vanished, though
> marble in Italy looked no more solid, gleaming in the quarries,
> veined with yellow, than the clouds over Park Lane.[1]

Necessarily her vision entails limitations. So strict a concentration on the aesthetic aspects of life involves a detachment of spirit.
Emotionally there is a sort of ethereal coldness about Virginia
Woolf's work. Imprisoned as they are in the enveloping garment
of their sensibilities, her characters are unbridgeably separate from
one another. They seem a little lacking in heart. And also in soul:
though, as she indicates in *The Years*, their creator had intima-
tions of an eternal principle of beauty outside the flux of mortal
things, to the characters themselves, life floats by as evanescent
as a shred of mist. This mingled sense of life's beauty and its
transience, gives her books a tragic undertone. Behind their surface shimmer lies the shadow of a wistful sadness.

Yet their final effect is not depressing. The only depressing books
are those that show life as worthless. Virginia Woolf reveals its
every moment as brimming with interest and fascination and
delight. While the sense that it is fleeting only adds a poignant
jest to our response to it. She teaches us to 'love that well which
we must leave ere long'.[2] Thus does genius turn to glory its limitations. Even her coldness serves to add a sea-fresh purity to her
vision.

And now war has killed her as it loves to kill what is precious
and irreplaceable.

NOTES

Edward Christian David Gascoyne, Lord Cecil (1902–86), critic and biographer, Goldsmiths' Professor of English Literature at Oxford (1948–70). Linked to the Garsington set, his ties to the Bloomsbury Group strengthened in 1932 with his marriage to Desmond MacCarthy's daughter Rachel.

1. *The Years*, 1910 Section, 3rd paragraph.
2. Shakespeare, Sonnet 73.

'A zest for life'*

ROSE MACAULAY

She felt, looking drowsily at the island, all those paths and terraces and bedrooms were fading and disappearing, and nothing was left but a pale blue censer swinging rhythmically this way and that across her mind. It was a hanging garden; it was a valley, full of birds and flowers and antelopes....

In the midst of chaos there was shape; the eternal passing and flowing was struck into stability.

These two sentences from *To the Lighthouse* express the two reverse processes – dissolution of the concrete into the dream, reformation of the dream into the actual and stable – which are so constantly at work in Virginia Woolf's prose. Dissolution into smoke, into clouds, into insubstantial pageants, into thin air; we are such stuff as dreams are made on;[1] at times this seems the burden of her thought and of her words; then life recalls the dissolving dream, the eternal passing and flowing pauses and shapes itself into the bright clear moment.

Perhaps this is only to say that Virginia Woolf was a poet, writing a poet's prose from a poet's angle, and at the same time a novelist with more than the novelist's zest for actual life and actual people. The two in her combine, as they have combined in few others. That fluid, darting prose, informed with light, shade, colour,

* 'Virginia Woolf', *Spectator*, 11 April 1941, p. 394.

stirred by a hundred quick, crossing currents that flow and interflow like deep blue shadows on a running sea, is the medium in which her human creatures swim and dive, iridescent fish, amusing and alive. For when one thinks of Virginia Woolf, either of her writing or of herself, it is first her zest for life in all its forms of which one thinks; little in humanity was alien to her,[2] and not much outside it. Her novels and her essays, even her reviews, are rich in the amused appreciation of people that is peculiarly hers. She has been compared to Sterne, and she has indeed something of his ironic humour, but hers is more fastidious and more detached, subtler and less robust. I do not know to whom she can be compared; her mind and method were unique. Comparing, instead, one of her books with another, one finds (in the novels) a more or less zig-zag advance from the straight novel (*The Voyage Out* and *Night and Day*) to the darting dream of *Jacob's Room*, the enlarged, brooding moment of *Mrs Dalloway*, the haunted poetry, shot with wit, of *To the Lighthouse*, the rich, fantastic masque of *Orlando*, cut loose from all conformity with novelistic form, the complete abandonment of externals for abstract pattern of *The Waves*, then a return to externality in *The Years*. Neither of these two last uses the in-and-out shuttling method of the other novels; neither is, I think, so characteristic, for it is this shuttling, this interflow of the outward and the inward, that gives her novels, and indeed her other books, their supreme interest.

It was partly this that gave her the personal charm she so preeminently had. Her talk had a quality warm and gleaming; wit, irony and learning lit an immense interest in people, a zest for information about them, a creative shaping of their doings and characters into gay chapters of biography. She liked to have about her varied and sometimes rather incongruous beings, bringing her, as she put it, stories from their strange, rich lives of fashion, wealth, adventure or crime; if they modestly protested that they had no such fine tales to tell, she put tales into their mouths. For it amused her to embellish, fantasticate and ironise her friends, as she embellished, fantasticated and ironised all she wrote of – a room, a lighthouse, a frozen river, a paper flower, life flowing by; nothing that she touched stayed dull.

Increasingly she disbelieved (she said) in written reviewing of contemporary literature, and advocated literary criticism by spoken word; her own verbal reviews to her friends of their books were brilliant pieces of analysis. But all her reviewing was a creative art; more particularly, perhaps, her reviewing of biography, for her gift was for making alive rather than weighing in critical scales. Biography was so naturally congenial to her that it seems odd that she had so far published only one full-length biography, that of her friend Roger Fry.

Was she a 'highbrow', of the breed that we have been told lately is in deserved eclipse? If she was (and really what can this mean except cultured, scholarly, fastidious and fine in mind?) she is a living answer to that philistine nonsense, lifting up against it the flag of unarrogant culture and the ironic view of life. People, she said, talked so much nonsense about 'Bloomsbury'. She chanced to live in Bloomsbury, as she had once chanced to live in Richmond, but she regarded herself, as she regarded others, as an individual, never as a type. Were such fastidious culture and creating imagination as hers to be in eclipse, one could but wait impatiently for the dark eclipsing shadow of the world to pass and let it shine again.

She has died at the height of her powers; her last book, finished but not yet published, is thought by some who have read it to be her best.[3] What she might have written later is uncertain, for she did not write to pattern; all she wrote had, both for her and us, the interest of a lovely exploration. The gap she leaves is unfillable, her loss (and now when so much else is on the way to be lost) intolerable, like the extinguishing of a light.

NOTES

Emilie Rose Macaulay (1881–1958; DBE 1958), novelist, essayist and travel writer. Although Macaulay published her first novel in 1906, she established her reputation mostly in the 1920s.

1. Cf. Shakespeare, *The Tempest*, IV.i.150ff (Oxford Shakespeare, 1987 lineation).
2. *'Humani nil a me alienum puto'* (I count nothing human alien to me), Terence, *Heauton Timorumenos.*
3. *Between the Acts* was published in July 1941.

A 'rare mind and personality'*

STEPHEN SPENDER

In these dark times, the death of Virginia Woolf cannot strike her circle of friends and admirers except as a light which has gone out. Whatever its significance, her loss is irreparable. Her strength – and perhaps also her weakness – lay in her rare mind and personality. Moreover, the quality of what she created had the undiluted purity of one of those essentially uncorrupted natures which seem set aside from the world for a special task by the strangest conjunction of fortune and misfortune.

Yet when one thinks of what Virginia Woolf achieved, her life appears far more a wonderful triumph over many difficulties than in any sense a defeat. In a different time or in different circumstances, she might well have died far younger and with far less finished. As it is, although she died at the height of her powers, she had completed the work of a lifetime. The history of other writers who have suffered from ill-health shows how much there is here to be grateful for.

Her best novels, or prose poems in the form of fiction, are *The Voyage Out, Jacob's Room, Mrs Dalloway, To the Lighthouse, Orlando, The Waves*. Although all of these novels have in common the qualities which distinguish her writing, they differ not merely in portraying different material, but in having different artistic aims. Indeed the artistic aims in Virginia Woolf's novels are far more varied than the material, which is somewhat narrow and limited.

Most novelists having achieved, by about their third novel, a mature style, continue to write novels in that style, but covering different aspects of experience. With Virginia Woolf, however, style, form and material are indivisible. With every new novel she was 'trying to do something different', especially with time. For example, the whole action of *Mrs Dalloway* takes place in one day; the first long section of *To the Lighthouse* describes a scene

---

* 'Virginia Woolf: A Tribute', *Listener*, 10 April 1941, p. 533.

lasting for perhaps an afternoon; this is followed by a very short section describing the passage of several years, illustrated by the decay of an empty house. *Orlando* is a fantastic account of someone who lives for several hundred years, beginning as a man and turning into a woman. *The Waves* is a poetic account of people seen through each other's minds through all their lives, speaking their thoughts in poetic imagery to each other. A new way of writing a book was simply a new way of looking at life for Virginia Woolf: she held life like a crystal which she turned over in her hands and looked at from another angle. But a crystal is too static an image; for, of course, she knew that the crystal flowed.

It is a well-known device of composers to take a theme and write variations on it. The same tune which is trivial in one light passage in a major key is profound in a minor key scored differently; at times the original tune seems lost while the harmonies explore transcendent depths far beyond the character of the original theme; now the tune runs fleetingly past us; now it is held back so that time itself seems slowed down or stretched out. This musical quality is the essence of Virginia Woolf's writing. The characters she creates – Mrs Dalloway, Mrs Ramsay, Mr Ramsay – are well defined to be sure, but they are only the theme through which she explores quite other harmonies of time, death, poetry and a love which is more mysterious and less sensual than ordinary human love.

A passage from *To the Lighthouse* will illustrate the peculiar beauty which she could achieve. Mr Ramsay, who is a philosopher – almost a great Victorian – faces the sense of his own failure:

And what are two thousand years? (asked Mr Ramsay ironically, staring at the hedge). What, indeed, if you look from a mountain top down the long wastes of the ages? The very stone one kicks with one's boot will outlast Shakespeare. His own little light would shine, not very brightly, for a year or two, and would then be merged in some bigger light, and that in a bigger still. (He looked into the darkness, into the intricacy of the twigs.) Who then could blame the leader of that forlorn party which after all has climbed high enough to see the waste of the years and the perishing of stars, if before death stiffens his limbs beyond the power of movement he does a little consciously raise his numbed fingers to his brow, and square his shoulders, so that when the search party comes they will find him dead

at his post, the fine figure of a soldier? Mr Ramsay squared his
shoulders and stood very upright by the urn.[1]

This passage has all Virginia Woolf's virtues, and perhaps some
of her defects. It starts off by being very faithful even in its irony
to the thoughts of Mr Ramsay. She takes one of those plunges
beyond the present situation of her character into the past and
the future which strikes one often in her writing as a flight of
pure poetic genius. But then the focus shifts and the writer has
forgotten her character's thoughts, or perhaps she is regarding
him from the outside. But the image of the leader of the expedi-
tion in the snow is a little too general, and one begins to wonder
whether she hasn't strayed too far from the particular.

As with the impressionist painters, there are opposing tend-
encies in her novels. The one is centrifugal, the tendency for everything to dissolve into diffused light and in the brilliant detachment
with which their surroundings flow through her characters' minds.
The other is centripetal – the tremendous preoccupation with form
which nevertheless holds her novels together and makes them
far more significant than if they were just the expression of a
new way of looking at life. This doubtless reflects an acute nervous
tension in her own mind between a too great sensitivity which
tended to disintegrate into uncoordinated impressions, and a noble
and sane determination not to lose hold of the central thread.

To have known Virginia Woolf is a great privilege, because it
is to have known an extraordinary and poetic and beautiful human
being. Some critics describe her as forbidding and austere. Her
austerity was not that of a closed-in or a prudish mind. As with
all genuinely intelligent people, one could discuss anything with
her with the greatest frankness; she was far too interested in life
to make narrow moral judgments. Perhaps she was a little too
impatient towards stupidity and tactlessness; it is a gift to writers
to suffer fools gladly. To be with her was a joy, because her delight
and her awareness of everything around her communicated themselves easily and immediately to her friends. What was written
on her beautiful unforgettable face was not severity at all, though
there was some melancholy; but most of all there was the devotion and discipline which go with the task of poetic genius, together
with the price in the way of nervous strain and physical weakness which doubtless she had to pay.

NOTES

Stephen Harold Spender (b. 1909; knighted 1983), poet, rose to prominence in the 1930s in the circle of W. H. Auden and Christopher Isherwood. Co-editor of *Horizon* and later editor of *Encounter*, he has also been a noted reviewer, critic and translator as well as an editor of literary anthologies and a frequent visiting lecturer in English literature.

1. *To the Lighthouse*, sect. I, ch. VI.

Remembering Virginia Woolf*

SIR HUGH WALPOLE

I read *Jacob's Room* for the first time in a Turkish Bath in Marseilles. I didn't open it until I had reached my warm, dry cubicle and been rolled and rolled securely inside sheets and blankets by the fat one-eyed attendant who was afterward murdered for raping the young daughter of the bath's *patron*.

All this may seem irrelevant now. It did not seem so then, for I was lazy and comfortable after my bath and not at all inclined for reading. Everything was then relevant. I looked up lazily at the one-eyed attendant and said: 'I feel in my bones you will be murdered one day'.

'Very likely, monsieur', he agreed, smiling.

It is my only successful prophecy. I must have slumbered, but later I awoke and began *Jacob's Room*. When I came to Jacob and the sheep's skull on the seashore I sat up, my wrappings falling from me, and I knew that I had found one of the books of my life. The books of *my* life are supposed by my detractors to be too many. They are not really so, but they are very varied and include *Vathek, Alice in Wonderland, Clarissa, The Prelude, Bleak House, Death's Jest-Book, The Woodlanders*, and *Siren Land*.[1] They have no reason – my likings for these particular works. They may be good or bad. *Jacob's Room* is one of them. *Orlando* is another.

No other of Virginia Woolf's works are in this personal collection of mine, although I think *Mrs Dalloway* her best novel, and

* 'Virginia Woolf', *New Statesman and Nation*, 14 June 1941, pp. 602–3.

The Waves her most beautiful poem. This reminiscence, however, is not to be about her books, but about herself. I mention my reading of *Jacob's Room* only because it was my true introduction to her. I had read *The Voyage Out* and some small things. Before the 1914 War I had been startled by reading that Mr Clive Bell said that there were three living English novelists who really mattered, and only three. One of them was Virginia Woolf. At that time – 1913 I think it was – this saying was a dark one.[2] I did not think then, I do not think now, that Clive Bell, a delightful writer and an enchanting companion, knew or cared much about the art of novel-writing. Nevertheless, his words had an oracular sound. Who then was Virginia Woolf? I read *The Voyage Out*. I was not greatly impressed by it. It appeared to me stuffy, laboured and derivative.

So it was that *Jacob's Room* enchanted me all the more by its surprise. I thought it marvellous that Jacob, who scarcely speaks from the first to the last, should be so intimate to me, and so endearing. It was this book, I suppose, that made me unjust to Maugham's *Of Human Bondage*, read by me at this time.[3] How melodramatic and cheap did it seem and still does beside *Jacob's Room*! When later than this I saw Virginia Woolf I was terrified. Literary ladies from Rhoda Broughton through Katherine Mansfield and Rebecca West to Gertrude Stein have worn, from time to time, the robes of priestesses engaged in throwing fragrant incense on to their own altars.[4] Katherine Mansfield's *Letters*, brilliant and touching, seem to me exactly to do this.[5]

Virginia Woolf had at that first meeting for me the air of a priestess, but a priestess who was at the same time for me strangely home-familiar. I mean that in her beautiful deep, slow voice, her delicate hostess care of one at the tea-table, her courtesies and dignities, she resembled many of my relations in my own youth – aunts and cousins; she was, in fact, a lady.

I don't know whether it is snobbery that comes in here, but I do know that I had been growing tired, for a long time past, of meeting so occasionally the beautiful courteous manners of my childhood. I had so often been told that they were stuffy, hypocritical and especially restricting to females.

It was pleasant to discover that Virginia, who, more than any other woman writer of her time, was modernist in her passionate championship of women, could not help but be courteous in the Victorian tradition even had she wished to. And she did not so wish.

As to throwing incense on her own altar, that was not at all the thing at this first tea-party. Virginia Woolf was ironic about her own work and delicately humorous about others'. I had discovered before this that Bloomsbury was not the mutual admiration society the outside world supposed it. Nowhere in Fleet Street had I watched so gay and ribald a treatment of Helen Schlegel's absurd baby from *Howards End* as in Bloomsbury, nor was Aldous Huxley's compassionate Encyclopaedia considered entirely serious in Tavistock Square.[6]

At that first tea-party in that little room with the Duncan Grant murals, the muffins and the two conscious, watching, over-hearing teapots I tasted the best honey of my life. And always, afterwards, up to a year ago, that honey was there.

Nevertheless, I was frightened. I was frightened, as it has been all my life my nature to be frightened, by people who think before they speak. I don't mean, of course, that that is a thing I never do, but words rush from me more swiftly than they should. Now Virginia saw folly more quickly than it flies and always she slew it without a second's compunction. Not fools, I hasten to say, but folly. Of fools she could often be exceedingly tender and she enjoyed them sometimes as friends.

My own fears increased with my own sense that I was not nearly such a fool as I seemed to be, and then there came a day when she attacked me fiercely for my printed praise of a certain novel. This was a mystical story concerned with death and poetry. Virginia attacked it on the ground of the insincerity of the author, whom she did not know. It was humbug; he did not mean a word that he said.

Now I happened to know the author, and I was certain that whatever else he might be, he was sincere. I told her some facts about him and suddenly her interest in the curious psychology of that author overcame all her dislike of his book. All she wanted was the truth and I gave her as much as I could of it. From that day I was never afraid of her again. I saw that if with her at least I was not a humbug, I need have no fear. I saw that her eagerness to know the truth was inexhaustible. In this she exactly resembled Henry James, whose curiosity about this strange confusion called life was without end. Virginia took your stories from you in two ways. Either she was gay and creative, would snatch something from you, make something charming, fantastic, beautiful from it, and then hand it back to you pretending it was all your own. Or, more serious, she would investigate and investigate, delving further and further – and then when you had given her everything you could, then would come that little pause, as it used to come in the old days with James, and that unspoken question: 'Well – is that all? Can't we find anything else? Surely you know that we haven't discovered the *real* pattern in the carpet?'[7]

Nevertheless, I told her more than I ever told any other human being, more than I shall ever tell any human being again.

Then it was that I discovered that beneath the mocking humour, the sometimes stern enquiry, the sharp wonder, the restless investigation, there was a kindness of heart and tenderness of feeling rich with an intense personal charity.

I remember my surprise at finding that she realised, better than any save my closest friend, the suffering that a truly fearful attack of arthritis caused me. We are, most of us, bored with the pains and agonies of our friends. At any rate, we cannot listen to tales of woe for very long. She did not say a great deal nor invite many details, but I loved her from that time.

I suppose then that all of us who were her friends feel a kind of bewilderment. Always when some friend leaves us in physical death, we realise with a new sharpness that *that* particular human being was unique. The uniqueness, while the friend was still here, was veiled. At any time we might see the friend again, write or receive a letter, have a message. The uniqueness composed of such various qualities had been sometimes annoying or boring or exacerbating. But now – how one longs for him to open the door, stand, smiling, in the doorway!

And if that is true of other friends, how poignantly is it true of Virginia Woolf! How, as I am writing this, I long to be able to go up the narrow stairs again to see that little book-bursting room, to greet the two intelligent teapots and hear that deep, lovely voice explaining to some other friend a foible, an absurdity of her own, of mine, of a stranger in the street.

Her loss is something from which I shall now never escape.

NOTES

Hugh Seymour Walpole (1884–1941; knighted 1937), New Zealand-born novelist, educated at Cambridge. Walpole was widely and well-connected in the literary scene of his day, counting Henry James, Arnold Bennett, H. G. Wells and Joseph Conrad among his acquaintance. A highly popular writer, his reputation fell into eclipse after his death.

1. Works by William Beckford, Lewis Carroll, Samuel Richardson, William Wordsworth, Charles Dickens, Thomas Beddoes, Thomas Hardy and Norman Douglas, respectively.

2. Walpole's time-frame is in error: Woolf's first novel, *The Voyage Out*, was not published until 1915.

3. W. Somerset Maugham's novel was first published in 1915.

4. Rhoda Broughton (1840–1920), novelist. Gertrude Stein (1874–1946), American writer.

5. *The Letters of Katherine Mansfield*, ed. John Middleton Murry (2 vols, 1928).

6. E. M. Forster's *Howards End* (1910). Huxley's work is presumably *An Encyclopedia of Pacifism* (1937), which he edited for the Peace Pledge Union.

7. Allusion to Henry James's short story 'The Figure in the Carpet', *Embarrassments* (1896).

Index